TONY MORGAN

KILLING COCKROACHES

AND OTHER SCATTERED MUSINGS ON LEADERSHIP

B&H
PUBLISHING GROUP

NASHVILLE, TENNESSEE

KILLING COCKROACHES
Copyright © 2009 by Tony Morgan
All Rights Reserved

ISBN 978-0-8054-4785-9
B&H Publishing Group
Nashville, Tennessee
www.BHPublishingGroup.com

Dewey Decimal Classification: 303.3
Subject Heading: Leadership

Printed in the United States
1 2 3 4 5 6 7   12 11 10 09

✦ ✦ ✦ TABLE OF CONTENTS ✦ ✦ ✦

✦ ✦ ✦ IF YOU'RE CURIOUS ABOUT ✦ ✦ ✦

✦ ✦ ENTER AT YOUR OWN RISK ✦ ✦ ✦ ✦ ✦

I remember the first time I had to stand in front of an audience and speak. I think I was in fifth grade. It was a gathering that included classmates, older students, and adults. I don't remember anything I said that day. All I know is I delivered my message, and at one point people laughed. If I was nervous, I've forgotten it.

One day recently I woke up in Phoenix. Later that day I was scheduled to deliver a keynote session in front of a large audience. The message was similar to one I've shared many times in the past. Crazy thing is that I woke up nervous. Thoughts rushing through my head. Racing heart. Sweaty hands. Guess I've learned fear. Sometimes experience stinks.

Regrettably, I have those same nervous emotions now because I know this book isn't for everyone. In fact, some of you are going to hate it. If you're looking for one message woven throughout twelve distinct chapters, you've come to the wrong place. If you're looking for new theory or deep theological discussions, this isn't your book. If you're hoping to find insights grounded in statistical analysis and confirmed through empirical research, put this book down and slowly step away from the shelf.

Killing Cockroaches is not for you.

A couple of my friends recently visited a grocery store to film a video they uploaded to YouTube. It was a no-budget film that lasted only a few seconds. In the scene, one of my friends said, "Take it like a man." Then he proceeded to grab a fresh loaf of bread and whack my other friend in the face.

Honestly, I don't know what that's supposed to mean. But it was funny. It was short. It was distinct. It was viral. And it got me thinking—these guys are idiots.

There are over one hundred stories packed in this book. Think of each of them as a loaf of bread. One whack along the side of your face may get your attention. Too many whacks at once will probably give you a headache. That's why I recommend you read this in small doses. Read a story. Let it settle. Decide if you agree or not. Allow it to spawn an idea or to generate a question. Copy it. Give it to a friend. Start a conversation. My mission is merely to get you thinking and hopefully to impact the story you are writing with your life and your leadership.

This book was nearly four years in the making. I'm certainly not expecting you to devour it overnight. Hopefully, though, you'll catch a thought that turns into an inspiration and prompts an action. And if you see something that you surmise was intended to be a joke, it's OK to laugh. That will help calm my nerves.

This is a book of small, simple ideas. If that's what you're looking for, you've come to the right place. Enjoy.

Tony Morgan
tony@tonymorganlive.com

In 1995, I stood in front of a gathering of people to share the vision God had given me for North Point Community Church. I told them that our community didn't need another church, but what we did need was an environment to which the unchurched would be drawn to hear the life-changing truth of Jesus Christ. It's a simple message. But as you know, building a church where people can hear that message is anything but simple.

Since that time, I've had to balance my limitations with my responsibilities as a leader in the mission God has called us to. It's God's church, so I am confident that his intentions will ultimately prevail. Jesus promised that even the powers of hell would not overcome his church. I sometimes wonder, though, if God knew there would be a day when I'd be a pastor and a leader. All leadership comes with responsibility. And, even though it's God's church, I have a job to do. Honestly, I haven't completely figured out my role in this gig. I'm still learning.

I don't think I'm alone. Be honest. Aren't there days when you just want to stick with what's familiar? I have those days. I want to do the things I know how to do with people I know. It's easier that way. The only problem is that safety breeds contentment, which ultimately limits the need for faith. We have to find that place of healthy tension between being confident in our calling and knowing that we cannot complete the mission without God's intervention.

Unfortunately our ministries can also become enamored with the familiar. Churches (really all organizations) tend to

TONY MORGAN

drift toward what's comfortable. Whether it's our approach to service programming or discipleship or teaching or any number of ministry functions, leaders must constantly battle the status quo. We have to challenge the existing process and identify new methods for fulfilling our mission. Yes, the message is the same, but we live in an ever-changing world. The language that we used in the past doesn't always translate in today's culture. And what works today likely won't work tomorrow. We can't let the church get complacent.

There's also the temptation to do church for those who are already going to heaven. You know what I'm talking about. If we're not careful, we'll begin to make decisions about programming and teaching to keep those who are *already* here at the expense of those who *need* to hear. That's not God's design. He wants us to communicate the fact that people matter to him. He wants us to talk that way and act that way and worship that way. It's counter to how we've always done church, though. It's also not easy. In fact, ministry to reach the unchurched is downright messy.

I'm amazed at how we tend to squander God's blessings given the certainty of his promise. We have faithful servants. We have talented people. We have financial resources. We have the power of the Holy Spirit. And yet, even with the certainty of the outcome, we fail to take the necessary risks to fulfill the mission. Remember the parable of the talents? God rewarded the two men who risked it all. At some point we'll all have to give an account for what we've done with our lives and for that which the Lord has given us. That includes our leadership and our ministries. Honestly, I think he desires to bless people—including leaders—who will put their faith into action and lay it all on the line.

I know it may seem like you've heard all this before, but let me assure you, you haven't. I came across Tony Morgan's writings for the first time a few years ago. I've read his books and I've been known to show up on his blog. In addition to being a gifted writer, here's what I've discovered about Tony—he brings a unique perspective to the mission God has called us to. He has a heart for the church. He desires to see people discover the life-changing hope, love, and forgiveness found only through Jesus Christ. And I'm confident he wants to see us revolutionize our approach to reaching a world that's open to spiritual conversations but is tired of the church.

Tony has been a follower of Jesus for more than twenty years and in church leadership roles for the last ten years. Early in his spiritual journey, God placed in him a passion for seeing the church experience a new relevance in the lives of those who are far from Christ. Tony doesn't settle. He asks questions. He learns. He challenges. And he shares what he discovers through his writing. This book is no exception. It reflects his heart, his insights, and his keen sense of humor. (Let me say, as an aficionado of the art of sarcasm, I'm certain you won't be disappointed.)

In *Killing Cockroaches*, Tony provides nuggets of wisdom about the processes and strategies we use. He reveals stories of people and ministries who share his passion for reaching the unchurched. He challenges us to embrace big risks in order to more effectively impact today's culture. If you're looking for a resource that will stretch your brain and your heart and your nerve, this is it. It may not be familiar, and at times it may not be comfortable. In his simple way, Tony has delivered a book filled with stories and insights that will make you look at leadership, ministry, and life from a new perspective.

Andy Stanley
Senior Pastor, North Point Community Church
Alpharetta, Georgia

✦ ✦ PREPARE FOR AN ADVENTURE ✦ ✦ ✦ ✦ ✦

You, my friend, are about ready to embark on a journey. It's going to take you to places where few people have gone before. You'll likely experience some turbulence, so fasten your seat belts. And if you haven't already, now would be a good time to identify the exit row closest to you.

You were made for this journey. You're a leader. A learner. A thinker. You're creative. You were designed for adventure. While others try to muster enough courage to embrace the reality before us, you're already considering where we might go next. Just in case you're wondering—I like you.

Some don't, though. It's not that they're trying to be vindictive. They just don't understand you, don't understand your value to the team. They think you're only there to cause disruptions. The fact is, we're all just wired differently. That's the way people are created. We're different. Because of that, sometimes people don't accept us. That's OK.

My desire is to keep things simple. That's the kind of guy I am. I have degrees. I've learned stuff. But along the way I've found that knowledge can get in the way. We can get consumed with knowledge. It can slow us down. Then one day when we least expect it, we arrive at the point where we think we know more than someone else. That's when we're dangerous.

You are a totally different breed. I can see it in your eyes. You understand, for example, that a corn dog needs both the corn and the dog. The two are inexplicably yet strategically linked. You're progressive in your thinking. You pave the way

TONY MORGAN

for new systems and innovations. We would still be eating our corn and our dogs separately if it weren't for people like you. You not only have knowledge, you're smart about it.

That's why I like you so much. You have ideas. You have passion. You have vision. But you also have this desire to encourage and equip the team around you. You don't want to leave anyone behind. That's admirable. I know it's also challenging—downright daunting at times. Don't worry. I've come prepared.

My title at NewSpring Church is chief strategic officer. That's what I do. I'm a strategist. My ministry is strategy. I teach about strategy. I write articles about strategy. I consult with other ministries about strategy. And several years ago, I launched a blog where most of what I write about is strategy. Recently I celebrated 1,000 posts on my blog. As that was occurring, I realized that many people, possibly those who needed it most, weren't getting the daily jolts of strategy insights I was sharing about ministry, leadership, and life. My blog readers, including a few thousand die-hard subscribers, were having fun and engaging in the dialogue. Others, however, including many who may still think blogging is a bad disease, have been left out of the conversation.

With that in mind, you and I stand at the beginning of this journey. Together we will delve into the inner recesses of my brain. Collected here for the first time are some of my favorite blog posts, magazine articles, and Web columns. Don't worry. Like a classic film, color has been added to offer a fresh perspective and new insights for those who have followed my ideas more closely in the past.

As much as I might not agree, I know there are those who don't embrace the credibility of an idea unless it's contained within the hardbound covers of a book. So here you have it. I guess some might argue a corn dog isn't a corn dog unless it's served on a stick. If that's the case, maybe strategy isn't strategy unless it's written in a book.

I'm not promising you'll agree with everything I share. To be honest, I hope you don't. Within these pages, though, I hope you find the inspiration to do something great.

FAQ
(That's "frequently asked questions" for those of you living in Belton, South Carolina.)

How do I kill cockroaches?

This isn't really a book about killing cockroaches. In this instance, "killing cockroaches" is a euphemism for responding to the *urgent* stuff in our lives that keeps us from doing the *important* stuff in our lives.

If, however, you really need to kill cockroaches, here are four easy steps:

1. Mix equal parts powdered sugar and borax in a bowl.
2. Sprinkle in cracks along walls and under cupboards.
3. Keep mixture away from children and pets.
4. Repeat as necessary for one to two weeks until all roaches have died.[1]

TONY MORGAN

Is a palmetto bug a cockroach?

One slight disadvantage to living in the South is the palmetto bug. Don't let the term fool you—it's a cockroach. They're very big here in the South. I'm pretty sure we could put a saddle on one and let the kids ride it around the house. You should see the process my wife and I go through to determine who gets to kill the cockroaches around here. I keep telling her she can take care of the cockroaches, and as a trade off I'll take care of every pesky rhinoceros that gets into our home.

Is this book only about killing cockroaches?

Well, in a way, I'd have to say yes. It's about a new way of thinking. The stories and strategies are intended to get your focus on the BIG stuff with small insights. There's actually only one story specifically related to killing cockroaches. Consider the rest of the stories insecticide to keep the cockroaches out of your life.

Does Orkin know about your book?

No. But keep in mind—purchasing *Killing Cockroaches* is a lot cheaper than it would cost for Orkin to come to your house and spray for pests. Therefore, I'm delivering knowledge *and* saving you money. With that in mind, maybe you should consider buying two copies—one for the home and one for your car.

Are there other options for killing cockroaches besides calling Orkin or buying your book?

Well, actually there *is* another option. The hedgehog is a natural predator of cockroaches. So you could purchase a hedgehog and let it roam freely throughout your home. Cats may also try to eat cockroaches, but cockroaches always make cats throw up. I'm not sure what happens when a cockroach tries to eat a cat, but I'd like to see that.

Does PETA know about your book?

I don't think so. But rest assured, no cockroaches were harmed in the writing of this book.

KILLING COCKROACHES (READ THIS FIRST)

I was sitting at the breakfast table recently with a bunch of guys and was reminded of an incident that took place at a former job. This was before ministry. I was a city manager—kind of like the CEO of a business. I was responsible for leading an organization with a big budget and lots of employees. I was the man. I wore a suit. Every day.

One day I was working at my desk, and I heard a woman scream from the other side of the office building. Just a few seconds later, the screaming woman ran into my office. She explained that she needed help. She had found a cockroach in her office. And for whatever reason, she thought this was a problem for the "CEO."

Remember, I was the guy who wore a suit. Every day.

I'm not sure why I did it, but I slowly pushed my chair away from the desk. Stood up. Walked down the hall. Entered the screaming woman's office and proceeded to

TONY MORGAN

kill the cockroach. I was wearing my suit, which, of course, I wore . . . every day.

It's been years since that incident. I don't wear suits anymore, but there are still days when I come home a little mopey. I guess the frustration is all over my face. My wife, Emily, will take one look at me and ask, "Did you have to kill cockroaches today?" But I've grown wiser about this. I've learned that there are things I can do to avoid getting stuck killing cockroaches. My responsibility is to move beyond just reacting to what's urgent. This includes things like:

- *Blocking time out in my schedule.* Actually setting appointments with myself to dream and plan and work on the big-picture projects.
- *Empowering other competent leaders.* Giving them significant ministry responsibilities and authority rather than just delegating tasks.
- *Identifying my strengths.* Positioning myself so I'm operating out of my strengths. And finding others who are different enough from me to manage around my weaknesses.
- *Hiring an assistant.* Not a secretary, but a leader and a project manager.
- *Surrounding myself with problem-solvers.* Not with problem-messengers.

I could go on and on, but the point here is: *I'm* typically the problem when my day is filled with killing cockroaches. It's easy to blame the screaming person who runs into my office, but oftentimes I'm the one who has allowed (and sometimes created) those urgent demands.

So the moral of the story is this: you get to decide where your time goes. You can either spend it moving forward, or you can spend it putting out fires. You decide. And if you *don't* decide, others will decide for you. Then you, too, will be stuck reacting to the urgent. You may not be wearing a suit, but you'll be killing cockroaches. Every day.

ACTION SPEAKS LOUDER THAN ADVERTISING

John at the Brand Autopsy blog (brandautopsy.com), wrote about how action speaks louder than advertising, citing the example of Wal-Mart's response to Hurricane Katrina. Their work received quite a bit of positive press coverage, including an article in the *Wall Street Journal*.[2]

I've found that actions speak louder than advertising in the "church business" as well. In fact, I think this strategy is outlined somewhere in our business plan.

"Suppose a brother or sister is without clothes and daily food. If one of you says to him, 'Go, I wish you well; keep warm and well fed,' but does nothing about his physical needs, what good is it? In the same way, faith by itself, if it is not accompanied by action, is dead" (James 2:15–17).

Isn't it amazing how truth is revealed? I think we even see it from time to time in corporate America. That's why I love the challenge of studying what's happening in the business world and filtering it through Scripture. There are times when I see something that really affirms God's design.

You can't buy the media coverage you'll receive if you remain faithful to God's design for the church and stay active in people's lives by addressing their physical and emotional needs. I've seen this happen in ministry with projects to feed the poor, provide housing for single moms, and many other missions efforts. It's inappropriate, of course, to minister to people with the goal of receiving good publicity, but don't be surprised if your ministry initiatives to help people in your community do generate a big story.

AGREE

The more I study the Bible, the more I find a connection between unity among believers and our fulfillment of God's will. Check out John 17:20–26—specifically verse 23. It says, "I in them and you in me. May they be brought to complete unity to let the world know that you sent me and have loved them even as you have loved me." Our efforts in ministry will fail unless believers are united in God's love and grace.

That's why I believe *agreement*—being spiritually united with Christ—in marriage, on staff teams, within a church, and in the larger Church impacts what God can accomplish through us. If you consider instances where you've seen division or brokenness in any of those relationships, you know that it dramatically impacts the fruit of our ministry and our witness to the world.

That's why it makes me so sad to hear Christ followers attacking other churches and leaders. Not only is it contrary to God's will for believers (some people would call it "sin"), it's negatively influencing the church's witness to the world. That's why I believe we, as leaders, need to:

- Pursue God's will for our lives and our ministries. (Col. 1:9–12)
- Deal with our own shortcomings. (Matt. 7:1–5)
- Embrace humility. (Phil. 2:1–11)
- Encourage others. (Eph. 4:29)
- Value reconciliation (Matt. 5:22–24) over division (Matt. 12:25).

In other words, it's God's will for us to agree.

ARE PEOPLE TALKING?

Recently I was reading the story of Jesus healing the man with leprosy in the first chapter of Mark. I've read that story a number of times over the years. In the past my focus was on the compassion Jesus had that prompted his healing of the man. This time, though, I was more focused on the response of the man who had been healed. It's interesting that Jesus told him to say nothing to anyone about what he did, yet the man could not contain his excitement. His life had been transformed, and he told everyone he met what had happened. This news spread all over the town. It spread so widely and so quickly that Jesus was forced to hide from the crowds.

It's pretty apparent that the ministry Jesus had while on earth created a lot of buzz. Word about what he was doing spread rapidly throughout the region. The questions that are raised in my mind are these: Do you think his ministry can still generate that kind of buzz today? What would our churches have to look like in order to transform people's lives so completely that their excitement could not be contained? If that happened, I bet crowds of people would begin showing up at churches.

Of course, you know what might happen—there would be curiosity seekers just like in Jesus' day. Some people would probably just show up looking for a show or expecting to see something dramatic. They wouldn't really be looking to enter into a relationship with Jesus. But I bet some of those people in the crowd would find Jesus and experience a changed life, just like the man with leprosy. And if that were to happen, it would continue to fuel the buzz.

Well, that was my thought process. And in thinking about it, I wondered if God is at all disappointed that the ministry of his church doesn't generate that kind of buzz today. I know. I should have just stuck to the "compassion" part of this passage. That's a lot easier to deal with.

AVOIDING MEDIOCRITY

NewSpring (newspring.cc) is a growing church. There are obviously a lot of people who love what we do. Given the number of people who have received Christ and been baptized and experienced new life in a variety of different ways, it seems the ministry is having an incredible impact. And we're grateful to God for every bit of it.

Of course, success, whether it's in the marketplace or in

ministry, seems to foster contempt. We're not "deep" enough. We don't offer this program or that program. We don't invest ministry dollars here or there. We're not Baptist enough. We don't use the right music. Our message is married too much to the culture. It's amazing the grief you get when your sole purpose is simply to point people to Jesus.

There are certainly some people who don't like the way we do ministry. Some are more vocal than others. It would be dishonest to say those comments don't hurt or at times cause anger. They do. But we learned long ago that to try to make everyone happy, you have to be comfortable with mediocrity. It's a place where there are few critics. It's also a place where few people become really passionate about ministry and their relationships with Christ.

Interestingly enough, I don't think God likes mediocrity either (see Rev. 3:15–16). I kind of like that about him. I think he prefers passionate people and churches with convictions and vision and purpose. I don't think he's looking for absolute perfection. If so, I don't think he'd like me. But I do think he's looking for passion. And I'm fortunate to be surrounded by that every day.

BAD WEB SITES

I spend quite a bit of time visiting Web sites from other churches throughout the country. In the process of trying to discover vibrant ministries, I find lots of uncool sites. With that in mind, I thought this list might be helpful. Want to turn your online audience off? Here are:

✦ ✦ 10 EASY WAYS TO KEEP ME FROM VISITING YOUR ✦ ✦ CHURCH BECAUSE I VISITED YOUR WEB SITE

1. *Avoid telling me what's going to happen at your church this weekend.* I found churches that had weather reports but nothing about their upcoming weekend service. I found two churches that had prominent information about upcoming golf scrambles (which, as a golfer, I appreciated), but nothing about this weekend's service. Why would I come if I don't know what I'm going to experience?

2. *Put a picture of your building on the main page.* After all, ministry is all about the buildings.

3. *Use lots of purple and pink and add pictures of flowers.* Really. Are you expecting *any* men to show up? And for my benefit, please don't put any doves on your Web site. Doves scare me.

4. *Make me click a "skip intro" or "enter site" link.* I don't have time for that and it's very annoying. If I have to wait for something to load or have to click around intro pages to get to the real information, I'm probably going to skip your church service.

5. *Add as many pictures and graphics as you can to the main page.* My life is already complicated. I don't have time to figure out what's important at your church. If you dump everything on the main page, I'm assuming *you* don't know what's important either.

6. *Use bad photography.* If you can afford it, hire a graphic designer and professional photographer

or purchase some stock photography, available at places like istockphoto.com. At the very least, find someone in your church who knows photography and can help you eliminate the cringe-factor from your site.

7. *List every single ministry you have at your church.* Frankly, I don't care what ministries you have. I just want to know whether or not I should visit your church this weekend. My first step isn't the men's Bible study or joining your church's prayer partners ministry.

8. *Make it hard for me to get directions, service times, or information about what will happen with my kids.* It's important that my kids have a great experience. If you can't convince me this will happen, I'm probably not going to risk visiting your service.

9. *Put a picture of your pastor with his wife on the main page.* That tells me your church is all about a personality, and I see enough of those people on television. I actually found a church that had not one but *two* pictures of the senior pastor on the main page. He was looking mighty dapper, though, in his fancy suit.

10. *Try to sell your church rather than telling me how I will benefit from the experience.* I don't care how great your church is. I just want to know if visiting your church will help me and my unchurched friends take our next steps toward Christ.

TONY MORGAN

Remember, your Web site isn't really for *you*. It's for the people you're trying to reach. They're trying to figure out if your church is a place where they belong. And if so, they want an easy way to figure out what they should do next.

BEING THE CHURCH

I saw it happen again with my own eyes. A NewSpring couple had a vehicle they no longer needed. Rather than selling it, they decided to donate it to the church. At the same time, a young woman in our church needed a vehicle because she was asked to return the car she had been borrowing. Today she received the keys to her new-to-her car.

I love watching the church be the church.

There's a passage in the book of Acts that talks about the early church. Among other things they were known for sharing everything they had. That same thing happens almost every day at NewSpring. It's one of the reasons I love my church family so much. It's a very generous community. Folks are genuinely interested in helping others. They live out what it means to love God and love others.

You ought to know that this characteristic of NewSpring's ministry didn't happen by accident. I've learned that a local church tends to model what its leaders value. NewSpring is a generous, sharing church not only because Scripture says we should be but also because Perry, our senior pastor (perrynoble.com), models this in his own life. I've seen him give away his own possessions. I've watched him push us to generously support various community organizations. I've been in meetings when he's championed the notion of giving our resources to other churches. Perry just has a huge heart for helping others.

If your church shut its doors today, would your community know it? As a Christ follower, are you generous with your possessions and your financial resources? I hope you have the opportunity to wrestle with these questions. I'm convinced it's a key ingredient to our mission as we bring the message of hope to our communities.

BETTER BLOGGING, 48 SIMPLE STRATEGIES

A close friend of mine is about to join the blogosphere. A blog, which is short for *Web log*, is just a Web site. Typically they are maintained by individuals rather than organizations. The content is usually posted in chronological order similar to a personal diary. Because it's on the Web, though, it's a very public diary. Believe it or not, there are more than 100 million blogs in existence with about 175,000 blogs being created every day.[3]

Here's the advice I gave my friend as he prepared to launch his blog:

- be you
- speak into people's lives
- keep it brief
- post regularly
- share the link love
- don't try to sell
- don't self-promote

- use humor
- be vulnerable
- build others up
- share your wisdom, but don't make me feel dumb
- celebrate success, but don't make me feel small

TONY MORGAN

- tell stories
- don't try to cover up your mistakes
- track your numbers
- don't obsess about your numbers
- comment on others' blogs
- monitor who is linking to your site
- talk like a normal person
- check your spelling
- tell me about your family
- find your voice
- find your audience
- focus on that audience
- tell us what you love
- offer your opinions
- don't spread gossip
- tell the truth
- spread the truth
- use lists
- allow comments
- provide an e-mail contact
- check your links to other sites
- develop relationships
- use pictures
- keep it original
- tease us
- remember, everything you write will be read
- don't publish everything you write
- pay for good design
- don't correct posts, except for typos
- update posts, but only sparingly
- don't ask me to link to your blog
- create conversation
- share what you're learning
- stick with it
- have fun
- again, be you

BOMBARDING PEOPLE

Trying to promote a new weekend series or event at your church? It appears that Wednesday and Friday are the best days to e-mail your audience, according to a report released by eROI, a leading e-mail and interactive agency out of Portland, Oregon. We also need to make sure we aren't trying to bombard people with our message. And the message better be relevant.

As the ClickZ Network reported: "It's possible for frequency or the messaging to push subscribers to unsubscribe. Sixty-five percent of subscribers said they unsubscribe when a newsletter is not relevant. Fifty-six percent unsubscribe to newsletters with too high a frequency."[4]

I think this principle works in other forms of communication too—including sermons. If we bombard people with a message they perceive to be irrelevant to their lives, they'll also unsubscribe.

BOOMER IN A GENXER BODY

In a dialogue on Todd Rhoades' blog (mondaymorning insight.com), Rick mistakenly had me pegged as a "Boomer." In actuality I was born in 1968. That makes me part of the Generation X. I've never understood that, though. I'm not really what people say I should be as a GenXer.

As I pointed out to Rick, I'm a GenXer who's optimistic about my future, committed to helping the institutional church reach more people for Jesus, and I prefer not to share conversations with complete strangers at the coffee shop.

I'm not a "slacker." I'm actually quite driven. I've had a job ever since I graduated from college. I've never moved back home to live with my parents, and I don't like to buy clothes from The Gap. (But I do shop at The Buckle.)

Makes me wonder, though, whether or not these generational stereotypes are really valid. Am I *that* different from my peers? Or when it comes down to it, aren't we really just wired differently by God? We grow up in unique environments. We learn through experiences in unique cultures. Maybe it's really not about the generation we belong to. Maybe God has just created us to be unique.

And if that's true, it'll probably always be the case that we'll need all kinds of churches to reach all kinds of people. We'll need seeker churches and emergent churches. We'll need small churches and big churches. We'll need charismatic churches and churches for guys like me who are, well, how should I say this . . . not very charismatic. I love that, though. Life would be pretty boring if every church was like my church.

And life would be very boring if every Christ follower was like me—a Boomer in a GenXer body.

BORING CHURCH SERVICES

One of the most frequent reasons people tell me they don't attend church is because the services are boring. I think the only place there should be boring churches is in Boring, Oregon, where I've identified (with the help of Google) that there are actually twenty-five Boring churches.

If I was intentionally setting out to create another boring church, though, this is how I might do it. Here are:

✦ ✦ 10 EASY WAYS TO MAKE ✦ ✦ CHURCH SERVICES MORE BORING

1. *Don't worry about when you finish.* I'm sure no one has plans after the service.

2. *Straight Scriptures, no stories.* Jesus didn't teach that way, but you're obviously a better teacher than Jesus.

3. *No television, no movies.* It's just a phase. People don't really need visual stimulation. They prefer talking heads.

4. *Use the same service order.* Every week. No exceptions. Ever.

5. *Make more announcements.*

6. *Encourage elementary school kids to sit through your services.* They love lively 45-minute sermons. It's good for them. It builds character.

7. *Talk more about the past* and less about the future.

8. *Use the same song every week.* And try the chorus one more time.

9. *Use lots of big words* that no one uses in normal, everyday life.

10. *Forget relevant topics and life application.* That's overrated. People are really only interested in hearing what you think, not why it matters to them.

OK, you probably get the point. The question is this: What are you doing to make your services memorable and impactful? Or do you believe unchurched people, people who aren't already in a relationship with Jesus, should just

TONY MORGAN

be expected to show up and put up with something they perceive as boring?

CHRISTIANS SOUND DIFFERENT

Kathy, over at the Creating Passionate Users blog (headrush.typepad.com), says that as we become more passionate about something and move towards being an expert on that topic, we begin to develop our own lexicon with specialized words. The words we use and the way we talk become almost like a foreign language to someone who is not familiar with the topic. She shares:

"Listen in on a conversation between three airplane pilots, and—assuming you aren't a pilot—you might understand 50 percent at best. Listen in on a conversation between three software architects, and even a new programmer might not have a clue. Snowboarders have their own terms. So do plumbers, photographers, librarians, ministers, dancers, realtors, musicians, graphic designers, and filmmakers (best boy? gaffer?)."[5]

Kathy is right. And when it's pilots talking to pilots, that's OK. When it's snowboarders talking to other snowboarders, that's OK. When it's musicians talking to musicians, that's OK. But when it's pastors or other Christ followers talking to people who are normal folks just beginning to check out the claims of Christ, that's not OK. When we speak our foreign Christian language, normal people don't understand. *Blessed. Saved. Witness. Born again. Grace. Blood of the Lamb.* These words don't mean anything to normal people.

My point isn't that we should dumb down our message (though I'm sure that's how others will interpret this because I'm a pastor at one of those evil megachurches that waters down the message just to fill seats). My point is that we can still talk about topics of the faith like atonement, incarnation, justification, redemption, and sanctification (see, I can use big words), but we need to put it in terms so that people who are just getting started can understand. Otherwise, they'll never become passionate followers.

Here's the reality, though. Christians *like* to use big words. It makes us look like we know stuff that others don't know. We feel more spiritual. For some reason I think it makes us feel better about ourselves. Kathy describes it this way:

"Think about it . . . come on, really think about it. Somewhere in your past (maybe even within the last 48 hours), you've felt that little ever-so-slightly-I'm-better-at-this-than-you feeling that came from being able to keep up with a book, speech, or conversation that had words and phrases not known to 'the rest of us.'"

Kathy is right. It *does* make us feel good. And again, when we're talking about flying airplanes, snowboarding, or music, maybe that's acceptable. When we're talking about the claims of Christ, though, that's pride and (consequently) that's sin.

I think it's time we consider how we're "equipping the saints." If we're just teaching people a foreign language, what have we really accomplished?

CHURCHINESS IS EASY

I love churches that aren't about helping people become churchy. Churches should be about helping people experience a transformed life in Christ that challenges folks to live out their faith daily in today's culture. That's a lot harder than just being churchy, quite frankly. Churchiness is easy. You just follow prescribed rules.

Real faith is dynamic. It's controversial. It's dangerous. It's constantly growing. It asks challenging questions. It involves mystery. You can't put it in a box. You can't keep it quiet. You can't outgrow it. You can't out-dream it. It's more focused on others than it is on itself. Real faith gives me peace but makes me discontent to let things stay the same.

It's amazing to see what God chooses to do through a church that embraces this kind of vision for life together. It's revolutionary.

COMMITTED TO COURTESY

I appreciate posts like these from ChurchMarketingSucks. com.[6] They were commenting on an article in the *Toledo Blade* about CedarCreek Church (aroundthecreek.com) in Toledo, Ohio. Their senior pastor, Lee Powell, actually has a marketing background and spent some time in the corporate office of Sears. Ironically, Lee and I have something in common. I also used to work for Sears, only I never made it to the corporate office. I sold socks and underwear in the men's department of the Sears store in Piqua, Ohio. Somewhere I have a badge to prove that I was "Committed to Courtesy."

The guys at ChurchMarketingSucks.com—(by the way, I agree that church marketing normally does)—pulled out an interesting stat from the newspaper article. CedarCreek church learned that 80 percent of their first-time visitors come because they are personally invited. Though Lee knows a thing or two about marketing, their ministry growth isn't from slick advertising. The church is growing because friends are inviting friends to weekend services.

There's nothing wrong with using marketing to raise awareness about your church or to create buzz about a series that's in your future. Go ahead and do the direct mailings to invite people to a new series and to get them familiar with your ministry. But when you mail out those postcards to the community, also give a stack to your people. Print extras so your folks can use them to invite their friends to check out a weekend service.

And when you have an occasion that requires fresh underwear, shop Sears.

COMMUNICATION LESSONS

One of the great opportunities I've had since joining the NewSpring team is getting an insider's look at how Perry prepares his messages. In the process, I've learned a few things and had a few other previous learnings reinforced. Here's some of what I've discovered:

- *Prepare your messages weeks in advance.* Tomorrow we're talking about the message for one month from

TONY MORGAN

now. You'd be amazed at what the Spirit will reveal in a month compared to a week. You'd also be amazed at what your artists can create to support your message with more time to brainstorm and execute.

- *Speak the truth.* The story is intriguing, but the message is dangerous. People want to be challenged. Deep down, we all crave truth. People will respond when we deliver the truth of God's Word. (This also assumes, of course, *you're* being transformed by God's Word.)

- *Keep it simple.* Perry teaches on one topic in every message, typically highlighting no more than three sub-points on that topic. The less you teach, the more your audience will retain and (more importantly) live out.

- *Sweat the outline and not the manuscript.* This is a new learning for me. When you sweat the outline, you pay more attention to focusing the content, providing supporting illustrations and creating a good flow. Because you're not preparing a manuscript, you also have more time to prepare/rehearse your message. And when you're speaking from an outline, you have more freedom to engage your audience.

- *Tell stories.* The story is just as important as the truth. This is the way Jesus taught. He used parables to reveal the truth. People will tune you out unless you engage their emotions. (By the way, take time to rehearse your stories. How you deliver a story is just as important as the story itself.)

- *Invite others into the process.* Perry talks about "evaluating the message on the front end." It's amazing what the team contributes by way of additional biblical content, illustrations, stories, arts elements, visuals, etc. Perry is a phenomenal communicator, but one of his secrets is that every message is prepared with the input of a team.

COMMUNITY?

Quick. It's a quiz. If I asked you how we improve biblical community (that's "fellowship" if you speak Baptist) among young adults, how would you respond? Home groups? Young adult connection events? Worship gatherings?

What if it doesn't have anything to do with those more traditional church programs but instead involves focusing more on how we interact in existing Web communities? Consider this telling quote from Experience founder and CEO Jennifer Floren:

"Over the past five years, the time students spend on the Internet has increased, which can be attributed to the fact that their behaviors online continue to evolve. As the Internet becomes more interactive, students no longer use it to merely surf or make an occasional purchase. Social networks have certainly contributed to this paradigm, and businesses are smarter about building sites that are more experiential and interactive and therefore stickier."[7]

How does the church tackle this new level of interactivity among young adults on the Web? Do we discount it and assume it isn't really biblical community? I think we're making a huge mistake if we assume young adults will continue to come to our buildings to experience community. If we agree

TONY MORGAN

that's the case, the challenge is figuring out how we embrace online social networks as a vehicle for biblical community. Is it the church's responsibility to corporately engage online communities? Or is there something we can do to equip Christ followers to engage these social networks on their own as they live out their faith?

If businesses are willing to become more intentional with their online strategies to engage students and sell their products, it seems like the church should be willing to do the same in order to encourage students to take their next steps toward Christ.

COMPEL THEM TO COME IN

Is your church service compelling? After all, our church services are competing with every other opportunity people have to invest their time. They could be reading the Sunday paper, sipping Starbucks coffee, golfing, sleeping in. We can shout the claims of Christ all we want, but if we don't compel people to come in and listen, our message is fruitless (see Luke 14:23).

I've found three key components to a successful weekend service that will compel those outside the church to come in and hear the gospel message:

1. *A relevant topic.* Jesus modeled this. In the Sermon on the Mount, he talked about real-life issues such as anger, sex, marriage, money, forgiveness, and fear. Unless people understand that Jesus offers hope

26

for the real issues they're facing, they'll tune out our teachings.

2. *A strategic theme.* It's not enough just to teach on a relevant topic. The topic needs to connect with a theme that's already captured people's attention. If the message or series theme relates to a conversation that people are already having outside the church, it's much easier to invite your friends. Package several messages around a culturally "hot topic."

3. *The biblical truth.* We can talk about topics that are relevant to people's lives and compel them to come in and experience a worship service. But if we don't offer them biblical truth, people will not experience faith and forgiveness. They won't experience the life change that happens when people redirect their focus and trust to the person of Jesus Christ. Romans 10:17 reminds us that "faith comes from hearing the message, and the message is heard through the word of Christ."

So here's the real test for whether your church is implementing these three components for a compelling service. Sit down with your service bulletins from the last six months. For each service or series, answer these questions:

- Did we address a relevant topic?
- Did we connect it to a theme that's hot in the culture?
- Did we offer biblical truth?

TONY MORGAN

Then track the attendance for each service. As you carefully review each one, don't be surprised if you see a pattern emerge. When all three components are present in a service, more people will be compelled to come into your church and hear the gospel message. And when you begin to see lives changed, you'll know your services are compelling for all the right reasons.[8]

COMPLEXITY CREEP

John Moore at Brand Autopsy had a brilliant insight concerning "complexity creep" that every church should keep in mind. He describes complexity creep as a situation where companies keep plugging in new things but never unplug old things, resulting in confusion with customers and employees. He described the complexity creep that Starbucks may be experiencing, for example:

"New beverages, new sandwiches, and new media offerings have been creeping into Starbucks stores and making a Starbucks barista's job exponentially more complicated than it was 10 years ago. The complexity Starbucks employees face on a daily basis ultimately impacts the experience customers have."[9]

Ever felt like you were battling complexity creep? Don't you wish there was a salve you could apply to get rid of it? Since there isn't, now would be a good time to stand at the whiteboard with your leadership team to develop a not-to-do list for your ministry. Here are some questions to prompt your thinking:

- What does your organization do that requires a major "platform" announcement in order for it to succeed? (If you have to manufacture excitement, it's probably something you should stop doing.)
- What events or programs would you not participate in if you weren't "required" to? (If the pastor doesn't want to go, that's another good indication you should stop it.)
- Where is the fruit? Would it be more abundant if you had more time, energy, resources, volunteers, etc.? (People will love you if you help them simplify their lives.)
- We're standing in line at Wal-Mart. (Your anxiety level is already rising, isn't it?) Let's pretend that I know nothing about your ministry. Before I pay for what's in my shopping cart, I want you to explain to me what steps I would take in your church to move from being a first-time guest to a fully-devoted follower of Christ. Ask yourself: Could everyone on your team pass the "Wal-Mart checkout line test"?

Your strategy should be so simple that everyone in your leadership core could rattle it off and those on your ministry fringe could easily pick it up. What are you doing to avoid the complexity creep?

CONNECTIONS

A reader from Ohio wrote and asked how we organize volunteers and whether or not there's a committee that helps with that responsibility. For starters, "committee" is a bad word around NewSpring. In fact, I think committees generally make it more difficult for people to connect in ministry.

In a former life, I attended church committee meetings. Lots of people sat around complaining about lots of topics, but very little if any ministry was accomplished. That's why at NewSpring we only have one board of lay people that oversees the mission, vision, and values of our church. Everyone else is volunteering on a ministry team. One big advantage of this decision is that we now have more people in ministry than in meetings.

Instead of using a committee, here are three good ways to encourage people to connect into volunteer roles:

- *Shoulder-tapping.* Ask people who are already serving in ministry to invite their friends to serve. Since there's already an existing relationship there, people are more likely to enjoy serving and to stick with it for the long run. As Tim Stevens (leadingsmart.com) suggested in our book *Simply Strategic Volunteers*: "If the pastors or church staff members (or committees if you have them) are the ones solely responsible for finding and placing new volunteers, then the growth of the church will be limited. All leaders and volunteers must believe that it is their responsibility to 'tap the shoulders' of the folks next to them and invite them into ministry."[10]

- *Promoting connection opportunities.* Offer first steps into volunteer roles through your Web site or your weekly e-newsletter. At NewSpring we don't promote many opportunities through the bulletin and we rarely promote anything from the platform. When we list available roles, the ministry teams are contacted directly (it's automated through the Web and newsletter). The teams take care of follow-up communications with the people who respond. They make sure those who have said they're interested are invited to an orientation, audition, or training session or are placed directly into a serving role. And depending on the nature of the role (like children's workers), there may be an application process and background checks before people can serve.

- *Providing a spiritual gifts class.* Take advantage of things like the Purpose Driven class materials that Rick Warren developed. His "Class 301" focuses on helping people identify their SHAPE (spiritual gifts, heart, abilities, personality, experiences). Once people determine their SHAPE, empower a team of volunteers to provide coaching on various ministry roles that might be a good fit. This team can also be responsible for follow-up to make sure people have made a ministry connection.

Whatever you choose to do, encourage folks to serve others either inside or outside the walls of your church. I'm convinced that one of the primary ways we worship God with our lives is by serving others.

CONTAGIOUS

Your attitude is your decision. And as a leader, the attitudes of those on your team are also your decision. There

TONY MORGAN

are many reasons why a positive culture is important to any organization, but one of the primary benefits is that it helps attract more positive people.

Steve Pavlina (stevepavlina.com) wrote a blog post on determining your "optimism ratio." He addressed this very topic. I love this quote in particular:

"You'll often see a pattern where like attracts like. Pessimistic news sources attract pessimistic readers, partly because those are the best targets for advertising—negative people are more likely to believe that buying products will change their emotional state. A pessimistic company will attract and breed pessimistic employees—the high-energy positive people will go where their enthusiasm is welcome."[11]

The lesson here is obvious for churches. If you want to create a contagious environment that's attractive to people outside your church, you have to build a team of cool, positive people. You gotta have fun, and it's your job to make sure your team embraces that value.

COUNTING ON YOU

Believe it or not, one of the most frequently asked questions I get is about the counting procedures we use to track our attendance. With that in mind, here's how we count at NewSpring:

- Our ushers go into the balcony and do a head count in each section of the auditorium.
- Some of the services are full enough that it's easier for

them to count empty seats. In that case, we subtract the number of empty seats from the total number of seats in those sections.

- The usher leader combines all the totals for each section into a spreadsheet at the end of each service.
- For children's ministry, we don't do head counts. Instead we run reports from FellowshipOne, the automated check-in solution we use from Fellowship Technologies (fellowshiptech.com). The check-in solution allows us to run reports that identify precisely how many children are in each room.
- Total attendance is determined by adding the number of adults in the auditorium to the number of children in our children's ministry center.

Attendance numbers are important for several reasons. For example, they help us monitor the health of our worship services. If attendance starts to plateau or drop, we want to know it so we can figure out what may need to change. We want to continue impacting people's lives for Jesus.

Monitoring trends also allows us to prepare for future growth with volunteer support, facility space, children's ministry, parking, etc. It allows us to be more proactive about how we're going to reach our community.

Additionally, it provides a benchmark from which we can monitor the health of the other ministries in the church. Our hope is that folks will be connecting in discipleship, relational, and serving opportunities at a similar rate to the growth we're experiencing in worship participation.

TONY MORGAN

Because of these reasons and more, attendance isn't the only measurement for church health, but it's certainly a key indicator.

COUNTRY MUSIC

On our way home from a Cubs game recently, we were listening to the radio. Between songs, the DJ mentioned that the two largest cities in the United States share a unique distinction. The DJ explained that New York City and now Los Angeles both do not have country music stations. I guess KZLA in Los Angeles changed to a pop format.

It had been quiet in the back seat of my car for several miles. Upon hearing the news, though, Jacob spoke up and said, "Dad, maybe we should move to Los Angeles."

This was a great reminder to "train a child in the way he should go, and when he is old he will not turn from it," (Prov. 22:6). I love my son. And I also love it that we share common disinterests.

It was also a good reminder to me that people, including my kids, are watching how I live out my life. Whether I'm conscious of it or not, my life is impacting the lives of others around me. The question, of course, is whether or not my actions reflect a positive influence that points people toward Christ.

I'm delighted my son has picked up a distaste for country music. I just hope the other important stuff sticks as well.

CRAIG GROESCHEL
ON KILLING COCKROACHES

BACKSTORY—Craig is the senior pastor of LifeChurch.tv. The original campus is in Oklahoma, but LifeChurch.tv is a multisite church with seven locations in Oklahoma, campuses in five other states, and an Internet campus. You can follow Craig and his ministry teammate, Bobby Gruenewald, on their blog at swerve.lifechurch.tv.

TONY: Tell me about an instance when you found yourself "killing cockroaches."

CRAIG: During the early years of the church, I spent so much time killing cockroaches I could have been an exterminator. I had to know everything, have my hand in everything, control everything. I inspected the bathrooms, proofed the bulletin, adjusted the chairs in the auditorium so they would be perfectly straight. Killing cockroaches was one of my greatest limitations as a leader.

TONY: What are some of the strategies you've implemented to avoid it?

CRAIG: John Maxwell said, "If someone else can do something 80 percent as well as you can, let them do it." I have slightly changed his number from 80 percent to 70 percent. I try to ask, "Is this the wisest use of my time for the sake of the kingdom?" If not, delegate. A key ingredient to delegating for me is not just to delegate *tasks* but to also delegate *authority*. If

TONY MORGAN

I simply ask others to do projects, they won't grow as leaders. If I put them over the projects and give them the authority to lead, they will grow.

TONY: What have you learned from some of these experiences?

CRAIG: Being too involved is one of the worst things I can do for our church. As a leader I am much more valuable when I have altitude in my thinking. This doesn't mean that I never serve others or do smaller tasks. It means that I don't live in the details and miss the bigger picture.

TONY: How do you help your team avoid "killing cockroaches"?

CRAIG: I think there are appropriate times to kill cockroaches. Someone has to! They are nasty! But if that is all we're doing, we're quickly losing focus on the true mission. Andy Stanley says, "Clarify the win." If killing cockroaches is what your ministry is about, then by all means, shoot them, squish them, and poison them. If that is not "the win," I'd suggest clearly defining what it is. The more passionate a team is about "the win," the more likely they won't stop for cockroaches.

CREATING BUZZ

Most people will attend your weekend services for the first time because a friend invites them. That means invitations are important. It also means conversations that precede those invitations are very important.

How do you help create those conversations? How do you generate buzz? By buzz, I mean all the dialogue that's created about the good stuff that's happening in your ministry. It's the accumulation of all the conversations that people are having in their e-mail exchanges, in the stands at the soccer fields, and over their venti caramel lattes at Starbucks.

As you consider the buzz that is (or isn't) being generated, it's important to remember your competition. If you're trying to reach the unreached, remember—your competition isn't other churches. Instead it's everything that's competing for someone's time and attention. It's the Sunday newspaper, a shopping trip, a tee time, the pillow after a night out with friends. What's going to grab that person's attention?

So the question is: How do we generate buzz about what's going on at our church? What we've learned is that buzz is created when we take an unchanging gospel message and present it using new, creative methods. When people who attend our services think, "This is new and different," they tell their friends. And then their friends talk—"Did you hear what they're doing over at NewSpring?" That's buzz.

The key to these conversations is the "new and different" part. When something is the same, it doesn't make headlines and it doesn't generate crowds. If something is creative and outrageous, people talk. That leads to friends inviting friends to come check out what's happening for themselves. You need to help fuel that conversation.

Being a bit different is an important ingredient to success. If people can't fairly easily explain what's different about your church, they won't be able to explain it to their friends.

Seth Godin puts it this way: "Something remarkable is worth talking about, worth paying attention to. Boring stuff quickly becomes invisible."[12]

We've certainly dared to do things a little differently at NewSpring. We've had the pastor teaching from a coffin. We've smashed cars on the platform. We tackle tough but relevant topics like relationships, sex, and money. Our services have had fire and smoke. We do these things to capture attention, raise issues, and provide a platform for revealing biblical truth. It's different. It's creating buzz. And it's helping people meet Jesus and take steps in their faith journey.

In his book *The Anatomy of Buzz*, author Emanuel Rosen described it like this: "Outrageous messages have a better chance of being heard than quiet ones." In encouraging us to be a little outrageous, he suggested we consider the "What will they think of next?" test. If the people you're trying to reach react with that thought, you can be guaranteed that you are starting to generate buzz.[13]

Here are a few things to consider as you're trying to take initial steps to generate buzz:

- *Figure out who you're trying to reach.* Then differentiate your methods to reach those people. Don't be different just to be different. Be different on purpose.
- *If you're different, some people won't like it.* When you're doing the same thing everyone else is doing, no one notices or cares. As soon as you become different, the message gets attention. You want attention even if it means some people will criticize your approach.

- *Different doesn't have to be big.* It could just be periodically launching a new teaching series that creatively ties the topic to something that is generating interest in the culture. Every new series, if done well, creates a new opportunity for conversation and buzz.

Let me just confirm for you that being different involves risk. As soon as you try something a bit outrageous, you run the risk that it may not work. We need to take that risk, though. If we don't, I believe we run the bigger risk that people will continue to view the church as out-of-touch, irrelevant, and boring. Don't let that happen. We have the opportunity to offer people unconditional love. Forgiveness. Hope. Purpose. Let's consider how we can capture people's attention and offer them the love of Christ. It's time we create some buzz.

DATE NIGHT SURPRISE

I took Emily out for some shopping and dinner the other night. The date was really to celebrate my recent birthday, but my idea of fun is buying clothes for Emily. We made our way around the mall to shop primarily for jeans and shoes, and that brought us to the department store. Emily and I selected a cool pair of shoes for her and headed over to the register where a nice, young girl greeted us and offered to assist.

As she began to ring up the sale, she said something that has become quite familiar to us through the years. Looking at Emily, she said, "You remind me of an actress." And like many people before her, she paused for a moment, and then it clicked. "That's it. Has anyone told you that you look just like Elisabeth Shue?" Well, the fact is my wife looks very much like Elisabeth Shue, which makes me just about the luckiest (that's translated "blessed" for the Christians in the crowd) guy around. And because my wife looks a lot like Elisabeth Shue, we have grown accustomed to this question.

Since we get this question so frequently, I've started to respond with a question of my own. I asked the nice, young girl behind the counter, "Who do I remind you of?" Again, she paused, and then she said, "Actually, you do remind me of someone." At which point, I started to get excited because I don't look like anyone. She looked for a few more moments, began to smile, and then exclaimed, "You remind me of my Uncle Dean."

I, of course, was devastated. My jaw dropped. I began to picture what I'm sure you're picturing. I thought, "If my wife is 'Elisabeth Shue,' I wonder what she's been thinking all these years being stuck with 'Uncle Dean.'"

Then the nice, young girl redeemed the moment. She explained that her Uncle Dean was asked to be a Gucci runway model. (For the sake of illustration, let's just pretend she was referring to the very manly version of the Gucci runway models.)

Needless to say, date night was a success. We walked away from our shoe purchase feeling very positive about our self-images. For at least one night, we were Elisabeth Shue and Uncle Dean the Gucci-runway-model-guy. It was a great reminder to me about the importance of speaking into people's lives.

Paul said, "Do not let any unwholesome talk come out of your mouths, but only what is helpful for building others up according to their needs, that it may benefit those who listen" (Eph. 4:29). When we practice this discipline, the person *receiving* the encouragement benefits, of course, but so does the person *communicating* the encouragement. There's a reason why Jesus told us to love others. It shifts the focus from ourselves to those around us. We are healthier when we move beyond the it's-all-about-me focus in our lives.

Elisabeth Shue and I enjoyed the rest of our evening. And whenever our friends need encouragement, we always recommend they visit the women's shoe department at the mall.

DAVE GIBBONS
ON KILLING COCKROACHES

BACKSTORY—Dave is the lead pastor of NewSong Church (newsong.net). The ministry has three locations in southern California and one in Bangkok, Thailand. The NewSong story is unique in that they've built a truly multiethnic ministry to reach their surrounding communities.

TONY: Tell me about an instance when you found yourself "killing cockroaches."

DAVE: Doing the normal church growth thing can be like killing cockroaches. Often our attention can be so given to building momentum and taking our churches to "the next level" that we may miss the outsider—the one who is different from us. It's the person who we wouldn't want in the church because he would make us uncomfortable and take us off rhythm—the proverbial Ethiopian eunuch rolling to a different beat by himself on a desert road, only on his way to impacting a nation for generations to come.

TONY: What are some of the strategies you've implemented to avoid it?

DAVE: I intentionally schedule time to be with people that aren't normal for me to hang out with both locally and globally. That includes making friends with international students at the local university. It also means forcing myself to work through junk with people I don't like.

TONY: What have you learned from some of these experiences?

DAVE: I've learned how much patience Jesus must have with me. It's been helpful for me to see God many times in the faces of those I wouldn't normally hang out with. That's given me a more holistic perspective of life as it relates to time, space, and relationships.

TONY: How do you help your team avoid "killing cockroaches"?

DAVE: I try to model it for them. I also challenge them to be the "neighbor." One way that really plays out is by doing vision trips with them to unlikely places.

DAVID FOSTER
ON KILLING COCKROACHES

BACKSTORY—David is senior pastor of The Gathering in Franklin, Tennessee, a church that's currently meeting in a movie theater. He's also written three books, including his most recent, *A Renegade's Guide to God*. You can follow David's ministry and life on his blog at davidfoster.tv.

My "killing cockroaches" story has to do with the issue of preparation. My life's calling as a writer and a speaker means I live in a world of words and ideas. This requires lots and lots of time in research and preparation in how to communicate your idea effectively.

I operate on one key principle—great speaking comes from the overflow of preparation. Before you can move others, you must first be moved. And that requires many hours of concentrated time, being still in one place thinking great thoughts!

Sounds simple—except when you realize that year after year the number one fear people have is speaking before a crowd. For me, the fear of speaking in front of a crowd isn't so great as it is speaking before a crowd unprepared. Therefore, I must spend hours and hours alone in an office in front of a computer, reading, studying, cross-referencing, researching, looking for illustrations, adding, deleting—all pointing toward one particular moment in which I will speak or write. I was taught that you need one hour of preparation for every minute you speak. That means if you speak forty minutes, you prepare forty hours.

Now here's my problem. I'm a guy of action and I live in a world of buzzers, bells, chimes, and alarms. They exist for one real reason—to get me moving! I like them because I love doing things. I love to be involved in conversations. When things are going on, I want to know about them. I want to do things that have an immediate payoff. But here's my dilemma: I get more immediate gratification "chasing the cockroaches" of my everyday interest or distraction. Hurry makes it easier to justify not preparing.

The truth is, preparation is hard, lonely work. It takes terrible inner discipline. It requires as much discipline to sit down, study, and prepare as it does to be actively attending meetings or dashing off to lunch, all of which feed the need for immediate gratification. So a lot of guys like me who speak for God week after week, year in and year out, face the urge to procrastinate on preparation because we want to be guys who do a lot of really important stuff with our time. Then we cheat on our preparation time and justify it by tending to all the small emergencies around us that make us feel significant.

If I'm going to be great at what I alone can do for my movement, I must guard my prayer and preparation time like money in the bank. Too many are in the habit of "winging it," thinking other people won't notice. But they do. We diminish our effectiveness by chasing a thousand little distractions. And who pays the price? The people who come craving an inspiring, insightful, and transformational message. So rather than preaching with power and conviction, we end up just recounting our "cockroach killing" stories, hoping our lame excuses will make up for our chronic neglect of doing the one thing only we could have done the past six days—prepare!

Who among us hasn't been on the receiving end of a boring speaker who was too busy chasing the urgent to invest the time it takes to be interesting. Talent can only take you so far. Preparation is what separates a good speaker from the truly great ones. Let other people put out all the little fires and chase the little foxes. If you are going to slay giants on Sunday, you must resist against the forces that distract, dissipate, and disappoint.

DEAL BREAKERS FOR LEADERS

Several of us had a great conversation recently related to the launch of our NewSpring campus in Greenville, South Carolina. We were talking about the importance of leadership development. After our conversation, these realities have been challenging my thinking:

- *Leaders can't be recruited from the platform.* We have to challenge them one-on-one. It requires a personal invitation.

TONY MORGAN

- *Leaders won't be fulfilled by performing tasks.* We need to give them real responsibility.
- *Leaders don't follow doers.* We need to make sure they're connected to another strong leader.
- *Leaders don't want to be micromanaged.* We have to eliminate the tendency to control the process. Instead, hold people accountable for the outcomes.
- *Leaders won't commit to ambiguity.* We need to offer a clear vision. And it better be big.
- *Leaders don't just show up.* We have to be intentional about leadership development.

John Maxwell challenged us all in his book on *The 21 Irrefutable Laws of Leadership* with this statement: "When a leader can't or won't empower others, he creates barriers within the organization that people cannot overcome. If the barriers remain long enough, then the people give up, or they move on to another organization where they can maximize their potential."[14]

Maxwell goes on to explain that it's only the secure leaders who are willing to give power to others. In other words, failure to empower other leaders is a sign of insecurity.

This stuff is smacking me in the face. How are my personal insecurities limiting the leaders around me? What changes do I need to make to empower new leaders? How does our ministry need to change in order to improve leadership development?

DEATH OF THE CHURCH BULLETIN

Do you ever wonder when churches are going to stop printing weekly bulletins? Do you really think people are reading them? I probably shouldn't admit this, but it's been months since I've read our own church bulletin. I use it to take notes during the message. That's it. Everything else that's in the bulletin is available whenever I need it in the weekly e-newsletter or on the church's Web site. In fact, I wouldn't be surprised if really simple syndication (RSS) feeds using feed readers like Google Reader (google.com/reader) or Bloglines (bloglines.com) will eventually eliminate the need for our e-newsletter.

Every organization has traditions that it holds on to, even though the purpose and benefit for which it was originally intended has waned. In church I guess we could literally call these "sacred" cows. We do it because we've always done it. At some point, though, you really have to ask: Are we still worshiping Jesus, or are we worshiping our sacred cows?

Oh, in case you're wondering, this section is not just about church bulletins. Is what you're holding on to as sacred as you think? Does it still add value? That's what it's about.

DEFINE YOUR VISION

Over my first ten years of ministry, I've been a firsthand witness to the power of a clear vision. I've seen how vision can bring about positive change in my own life. I've also witnessed the changes in hundreds of others' lives. Yes, along the way, I've certainly recognized that some of what has happened has been purely "a God thing." However, I've also seen how God blesses those who strive to discern his will for their ministry and then purposefully work to see that vision become reality.

I love the promises in Proverbs related to this. It's evident that God designed us to operate with a goal in mind and then to be purposeful in fulfilling that mission. For example, Proverbs 14:8 states, "The wisdom of the prudent is to give thought to their ways." Proverbs 14:15 says "a prudent man gives thought to his steps." Our call is to discern precisely what steps God has for our ministry and our lives because "many are the plans in a man's heart, but it is the Lord's purpose that prevails" (Prov. 19:21). And once we've identified God's purpose for our lives, we can be assured that "the plans of the diligent lead to profit" (Prov. 21:5). It's clear. God wants us to determine the plan he has for our ministry, and then he wants us to be diligent in seeing that vision fulfilled.

There are, of course, a number of advantages to establishing the vision and values of your church. A clear vision:

- *Sets expectations and fosters unity.* As an example, part of NewSpring's vision is that we'll engage the culture and enlarge the kingdom. When people connect with our church, they know that we intend to grow. We never have to revisit whether or not growth will happen at NewSpring, because we've decided it in advance and defined a vision that reflects that desire.
- *Helps facilitate decision-making that impacts our future.* There's intentionality to everything we do. To

be a growing church, we know we need to expand our volunteer teams, our facilities, and our leadership core. This means we need to make decisions today that help us fulfill our vision in the future.

- *Creates a framework for defining priorities.* There are a variety of valuable ministries that your church could implement. A clear vision helps you decide what ministries to pursue and what ministries to leave for someone else to tackle. With limited resources and energy, you can't do everything. It's better to determine where God has best positioned your church to have success and to focus your ministry efforts in those areas.

- *Attracts talent and financial resources.* People will give their time and money to a big vision. If you're finding it a challenge to attract either in your ministry, you may have to revisit your vision for the future. Do you have a God-sized vision? Is it big enough to get people excited about how they invest their gifts and time at your church? Is it big enough that it requires lots of prayer and a move of God to see success?

- *Defines success for your ministry.* Agreeing on a destination allows you to empower others to lead and carry out ministry. Additionally, it gives everyone a "scoreboard" to watch. It's easier to get everyone to pull in the same direction if there's agreement on what you're hoping to accomplish as a ministry. If you have a goal, it also makes it easier to celebrate along the way as you move toward fulfillment of the vision.

I can say with confidence that a clear vision makes a big difference. Without it we tend to get busy doing lots of stuff that may or may not be effective in helping people take their next steps toward Christ. Even worse, it gives the loudest person the opportunity to decide what does or doesn't happen at your church. That's how churches divide.

If you want to create an environment characterized by momentum, unity, and happy people, determine what God wants your church to be—now and in the future. This begins by establishing a solid vision and agreeing on the basic values that define your ministry. God wants that for your church.

DINO RIZZO
ON KILLING COCKROACHES

BACKSTORY—Dino is lead pastor of Healing Place Church (healingplacechurch.org) in Baton Rouge, Louisiana. Healing Place has multiple campuses across the Baton Rouge area with ministries that are focused on being a healing place for a hurting world.

Early on in our existence as a church, we were blessed to have relationships with some great organizations that would regularly send us truckloads of food to distribute to the community. We quickly went from a church with a pantry to a city-wide food distribution operation. In our context here in Louisiana, where there is a lot of poverty, this was a huge opportunity for us as a church to serve.

In my excitement, I wanted to do it all. I drove the forklift, pulled the pallet jack, did the paperwork, loaded groceries into cars, and coordinated shipment schedules. Our church parking lot had 40,000 pounds of pineapples on it at one point. In one summer we were given more than a quarter of a million bottles of Snapple for the needy.

I was so excited about what was going on. In one three-week span, we received and distributed 220,000 pounds of bananas. We learned very quickly that we would not be able to deliver such amounts directly to needy people, so we began connecting with other local churches and organizations—giving them the food for them to in turn relay to needy people. It quickly grew to 143 different groups coming to pick up whatever we had been given to distribute. But I soon found myself to be a bottleneck in the operation. I was a bottleneck on the forklift. I bottlenecked the paperwork. And I realized that although I was very active and engaged, I was not doing what I was gifted at doing. The relationships with the people giving us the food needed my attention. The groups we were relaying stuff to needed my time. I was more valuable connecting with these people than I was driving the forklift (as much as I loved driving it). And I needed to be the one ensuring the integrity of the distribution— that the gift was being given as it was intended.

For me, "killing cockroaches" was actually something I thoroughly enjoyed. But it was not the best use of my energy. I needed to empower others to drive the forklift (step on a roach) so I could do what I needed to do—even though I enjoyed the roach-killing.

My strategy was, first of all, to give someone else the keys to the forklift, then ban myself from the parking lot and turn in my work gloves (with a tear in my eye). I quickly learned that there were others who were better at driving a forklift than I was. And I found out that my gift was more along the lines of encouraging and developing the relationships that kept the food coming, and connecting to the people we were relaying it to.

At Healing Place Church, our staff is constantly reminded to keep in focus the need to empower others—to continually build and strengthen up relationships. We also do our best to watch for people who are killing roaches but don't have a roach-killing license. If someone is killing roaches but really should be doing something else, we try to recognize it and make a positive change in the situation. Lastly, we continually remind our staff that we can never hold our areas hostage. Whatever your area of responsibility, do not hold on to it so tightly that someone else cannot help you do it—or even do it *for* you so that you can move on to something else.

I see my own part in the work of ministry to be aggressively getting done whatever I need to do so that volunteer leaders can actually do the direct outreach with people. In the end, this lets me see that because I do what I do, many more people are reaching out and even more are being reached.

DISNEY

I recently visited Disney's Epcot Center in Orlando, Florida. First time there. Here are some observations from my day with Mickey and his friends.

✦ ✦ 10 THINGS I'LL REMEMBER AFTER VISITING DISNEY ✦ ✦

1. The experience begins in the parking lot.
2. We will invest a lot of money to make dreams come true.
3. It helps to have someone with you who's been there before.
4. The value of excellence transcends socioeconomic and cultural barriers.
5. It's hard to communicate with people who wear masks.
6. The journey is more fun when you're on it with friends.
7. The world is small.
8. Lots of people fulfilling the same mission can achieve great results.
9. It's possible to leave behind a lasting legacy for future generations.
10. We remember the fireworks at the end.

TONY MORGAN

DISTINCTIVE

My family and I are *American Idol* junkies. The six of us will gather in our family room to watch the process of winnowing the contestants from the tens of thousands of people who audition in cities across the country to the final show where America decides the new idol. We love listening to the singing, but we also love watching the stories unfold.

What we've learned in watching *American Idol* through the last few years is that it's not just about the singing. The quality of the voice doesn't necessarily mean a contestant is going to stand out. Sometimes it has to do with their appearance. Sometimes it has to do with their attire. Sometimes it has to do with their personality. Sometimes it has to do with how they move to the music. And, yes, how well they can sing also counts. But the bottom line is that there's a lot that the judges (and ultimately the American voters) consider when trying to determine the next American Idol. Just because you are a great vocalist doesn't necessarily guarantee that your voice will be heard in Hollywood.

Whether it's music or the marketplace or ministry, standing out from the crowd impacts our ability to make sure our voice is heard. William C. Taylor and Polly LaBarre expressed it this way in their book *Mavericks at Work*:

"When it comes to thriving in a hypercompetitive marketplace, 'playing it safe' is no longer playing it smart. In an economy defined by overcapacity, oversupply, and utter sensory overload—an economy in which everyone already has more than enough of whatever it is you're selling—the only way to stand out from the crowd is to stand for a truly distinctive set of ideas about where your company should be going." They went on to explain, "Mavericks do the work that matters most—the work of originality, creativity, and experimentation."[15]

Churches face the same challenge. In our situation, though, we aren't competing with other churches for the attention of our audience. Instead we're competing against everything else our culture throws at us that holds people's attention—everything from pop culture to careers to online communities to recreational activities and more. Talk about sensory overload—it's no wonder people are tuning out what the church has to say.

Here's the reality: our message doesn't change. We still offer the gospel. It's the truth. It transforms. However, the methods we use must continue to change in order to reach this "economy" in which people assume they don't need what we're "selling." Are you "truly distinctive"? It might be a good question for your ministry team to wrestle with as you try to make sure your voice is heard and the good news is shared.

DRIVE THE CAR

I recently gathered with a group of guys for breakfast and to talk about leadership. One of the guys was talking about the challenges he and his wife have faced in recent months with their marriage. We all face those challenges. No marriage is immune. He's married to a very wise woman, though. His wife suggested that she was getting really tired of talking about all the things they needed to fix in their marriage. She was tired of all the discussion.

She went on to liken their marriage to owning a car that's always in the garage. You get in the car. Sometimes you even start the engine. Most times, though, the car is up on the lift so you can tweak and tinker with it. You own the car, but you're always under the hood trying to analyze what's wrong with it and what needs to be fixed. One day she said, "I'm tired of trying to figure out how we need to fix the car—I just want to drive it."

That's powerful. And the thought occurred to me: this is a leadership lesson. If God has gifted you as a leader, then you need to lead. You can *read* about leadership. You can *talk* about leadership. You can go to leadership conferences and hear men and women share their greatest leadership lessons. You can analyze your leadership ability, and others can help you tweak your leadership skills. All of that is worthless, though, unless you eventually get behind the wheel and drive the car. Leaders will never become leaders unless they actually *lead*.

So here's my question for you: Are you a leader? If so, who are you leading? And where are you taking them? Are you surrounding yourself with other leaders? Do they ever get a chance to drive the car? Are they honestly allowed to drive, or do you find yourself sitting in the back seat telling them how to do it? Turn here. Turn there. Slow down. Stay in the right lane.

Here's the deal. Leaders want to know how the car they've been tinkering with will handle when they actually get it out on the highway and start driving it fast. Imagine owning a BMW that you never take out of the garage! That's how the leaders on your team feel when they never have the opportunity to lead.

So where are you? If you're a leader, are you leading? Are you allowing leaders around you to lead? At some point, you need to get the car off the lift and drive it.

EMBRACING CHANGE

When I was working in local government, it was displayed on the wall in my office at city hall. For the last several years, it's been hanging over my desk at home. It's just a simple statement I framed to be a regular challenge for me in my leadership. It's this quote from Sir Francis Bacon: "If we are to achieve results never before accomplished, we must expect to employ methods never before attempted."

It's so true, isn't it? Yet churches in particular have a rich history of hoping (even praying) for different results while clinging to the same ministry approach they've used for years. In some places it's church circa 1950. In others, the church is stuck in the eighties and it's considered "contemporary." Of course, if you're going to be stuck in any decade, the eighties are a pretty good place to be stuck. After all, it's the decade that gave us break dancing, parachute pants, and the mullet hairstyle. Those were great days.

The fact is—change is hard. Even if it's a good change, change is hard. Without working through the difficult challenges of pursuing positive change, though, we're missing

TONY MORGAN

out on the opportunities that might bring something new to our churches—new families, new faith, new hairstyles.

God loves the fresh and the new. He has promised us that he has new plans for our lives and our ministry: "Forget about what's happened; don't keep going over old history. Be alert, be present. I'm about to do something brand-new. It's bursting out! Don't you see it? There it is! I'm making a road through the desert, rivers in the badlands" (Isa. 43:18–19 MSG). I love serving Jesus because I know he's always ready to do something new . . . if I don't get in the way.

So what does it take to encourage an environment that fuels innovation? How do we develop a culture where positive change is both expected and embraced? It begins by shifting what we value. Churches that embrace change value some things over others. Organizations that are constantly on the cutting-edge of innovation:

- *Value mission over methods.* It's about fulfilling purpose rather than preserving traditions. We can't be married to the ministry methods. The message doesn't change. The mission shouldn't change. But the methods must always change. Otherwise, the church becomes irrelevant to people's lives.
- *Value people over programs.* Instead of filling the calendar with programs and events, churches will ask: "How can we help as many people as possible move into a vibrant relationship with Jesus and then help them share life with others?" Relationships require time. So rather than just *taking up* time, the church may have to

stop some programs to focus on what's most helpful for allowing people to move into healthy relationships both inside and outside of the church.

- *Value innovative breakthroughs over incremental improvements.* Incremental improvements are good, but if you focus solely on getting better or getting more efficient, you'll always do what you've always done. In other words, you can't just focus on efficiencies. You need to ask: "How can I get people's attention so that the message will be heard?"

- *Value risk over safety.* We have to give people freedom to fail. An organization that never changes and always tries to keep people comfortable and happy is far more susceptible to failure. We need to reward people for taking risks, even if they sometimes fail.

- *Value superteams over superstars.* A team generates better ideas and delivers better results every time. There's a lot of power in "we." When it's "our" change, it's easier to implement. Never do ministry alone. You need other people to challenge your ideas and make them better.

- *Value empowerment over control.* Change will flow naturally when we empower people to create rather than telling them what to do. When that filters throughout the entire ministry organization, look out! It's amazing what happens when people stop looking to the top of the organization for direction and instead start looking out of the organization and asking, "How can we help people experience life change through Jesus Christ?"

TONY MORGAN

- *Value action over analysis.* We can spend so much time trying to develop the perfect solution or strategy (or more likely focus on all the reasons why it won't work) that we never actually move forward. Just try it. If it doesn't work, stop it. Analysis still has an important place in every ministry, but we need to find the right balance between facts and faith and let God lead us into uncharted waters.

Are you ready to achieve results never before accomplished? I think that's what God has in mind for us. We have the opportunity to impact our communities by offering people a transformed life through the grace and love of Jesus Christ. There's power in that message of hope, but it won't be heard and people will not respond if we're unwilling to change how we deliver it.

God has given us "a new teaching" (Mark 1:27), encouraging us to use "new wineskins" (Matt. 9:17). If we want to experience something new and different in our churches, then we need to employ methods never before attempted. We need to be willing to change.

EVANGELISTIC ENEMY?

As a pastor, I want people to become Christ followers. I want them to fall in love with God's Word and experience the joy of gathering with other believers in both home groups and corporate worship. And I want to see their fulfillment in finding a place to serve in ministry.

But I face a big challenge because every time Christians step inside a church, it can remove them from the very place where they have the greatest impact for God's kingdom—the world. It's sad, but I wonder if we've inadvertently designed our ministries to isolate Christians from the places where God really wants them to be. Are we truly engaged in his Great Commission if every extra moment of our lives is spent at church?

I hear the way Christians talk. They want more opportunities to gather for worship. They want more programs to meet other Christ followers. They want more Bible studies to help them go deeper in God's Word. There's nothing inherently wrong with these desires. But what's often missing is a desire to see people outside the church commit their lives to following Jesus. As Christians, we can become so focused on our own faith journey that we forget God's command to go tell others the good news.

As a church leader, are you being intentional about the way you encourage your congregation to leave the building and reach out to others? Ask yourself these four key questions to find out:

1. What does a "good Christian" look like at my church? Am I asking people to do so much that they have no time for real life outside the church walls?

2. Am I making it easy for people to invite their friends to attend a service, participate in a home group, or engage in ministry to others? Am I strategic about encouraging people to reach out to their friends?

TONY MORGAN

3. Have I made it a priority to teach people how to develop relationships with people outside the church? Do my church members know how to share their story of faith? Do they pursue conversations that allow them to hear the life stories of those they're trying to reach?
4. Is my leadership team modeling outreach in their lives? Are they being intentional about developing relationships with people who haven't yet committed their lives to Christ?

Recently at NewSpring, we took some time to talk about these questions. During one of our subsequent weekend services, we asked folks to consider who in their lives they'd like to see accept Christ. Then using markers we provided, they wrote the names of those people on the walls in our auditorium. Yes, eventually we'll have to repaint the walls, but this helped people visualize the reality that being inside the church building is not the priority—building the church by reaching our friends for Jesus is the priority.[16]

EXCEEDING EXPECTATIONS

I drive a ten-year-old car. It's a good car. It gets me from here to there . . . most of the time. The best part, of course, is that it's paid for. The disadvantage to driving a ten-year-old car is that it periodically breaks down. Most recently, it was one of the fuel injectors that went bad. In order to get the problem fixed, I unfortunately ended up visiting two different garages.

The first garage I visited was a pit. Junk cars were sitting around the lot. Car parts were piled inside, and it had been years since anyone had thought to clean. The day I dropped off my car, they had me sit in the waiting room. The furniture they had assembled looked like found treasures someone had collected from other people's trash piles. The room was filthy and was being warmed by a portable heater. It took two days before I got my car back—and the problem wasn't fixed.

The second garage I visited was entirely different. It was super clean. Everything was very organized and the floors were obviously mopped daily. It was spotless. They had coffee and a morning newspaper available for me while I waited for their initial analysis. After they decided what needed to be repaired, they offered a driver to take me to work and pick me up when the work was completed.

Both businesses repaired cars, but my impressions of the two were completely different. Those same impressions will certainly impact my decision in the future when my car needs to be repaired.

As a consumer, I'm making choices every day about who repairs my car, where I shop for clothes, and what restaurants I visit with my family. You're also a consumer. And whether you like it or not, every first-time guest who visits your church is a consumer. Not only that, they remain consumers until they're convinced they should become a learner or a worshiper or a servant.

The first time people visit your church, it's unlikely they'll decide to give their lives to Christ and experience immediate life transformation. Instead, their primary decision is whether

TONY MORGAN

or not they're going to return the following weekend. Since that's the primary decision facing first-time guests, one of our goals as ministry leaders is to make sure that the entire guest experience says, "We're glad you decided to join us. We were expecting you. You matter to us and, more importantly, you matter to God."

With that in mind, we need to remove all the barriers that could potentially keep someone from returning to hear the hope found in Jesus Christ. We need to beat the competition. Again, the competition isn't the church down the street. The competition is any other recent experience your guests have had. That experience sets the expectations for what they'll experience at your church. Your competition is the mall, the restaurant, the theatre, and the garage with the fresh coffee and morning newspaper. These businesses have learned that in order to sell their products and services, they have to pay attention to the entire customer experience.

What we're offering is much more important than clothing, food, or coffee. Our business is introducing people to the unconditional love of Jesus Christ. We're offering people a new life filled with purpose and joy. Because of that, we should be just as committed as local businesses are in making sure our guests feel valued. We want them to return.

At NewSpring we've learned that the first moments someone sets foot on our campus are critical to whether or not they're going to connect with our ministry. Because of that, it's our goal for people to have a positive experience before they even hear the opening song in the service. Here are some ways we try to meet that objective:

- We try to maintain our facility in excellent condition. No water stains on the ceiling tiles. No coffee spills on the carpeting.
- We have teams of traffic people helping vehicles enter and exit the campus and directing people to open parking spots.
- In rainy weather, there are volunteers who will stand at the drop-off area with umbrellas in hand, ready to walk our guests to the front door.
- There are lots of smiling volunteers to greet people and to provide personal attention to guests by escorting families to our children's center and orienting guests to the church.
- We brew great coffee and encourage connection and conversation before and after the services.
- We offer experiences for children that are designed to capture their hearts and imaginations so that we have the opportunity to introduce them to Jesus.

Someone who has led the conversation on this "exceeding expectations" topic is Mark Waltz (becausepeoplematter. com), pastor of connections at Granger Community Church (gccwired.com) in Granger, Indiana. Churches from throughout the country have visited Granger to hear Mark talk about their "first impressions" strategies. If you can't get to Granger to experience it firsthand, I'd encourage you to pick up Mark's book, *First Impressions: Creating Wow Experiences in Your Church*, to learn more about how to create a church that's welcoming for guests.

TONY MORGAN

Why do we try so hard to exceed the expectations of our first-time guests? It's because we want them to know they matter to us before they hear that they matter to God. In doing so, it's our prayer that people will experience transformation through a new life in Christ.

FANCY GADGETS

I have a big aversion to hugging other people (especially other men), but I want to give Scott Rodgers, asociate campus pastor at LifeChurch.tv's Edmond, Oklahoma, campus, a big hug. His post on innovation is stellar. Scott shares:

"Create memorable experiences. Step outside the norm. Do it regularly. That's innovation. Give your people a story to tell around the water cooler on Monday morning."[17]

Innovation isn't about razzle-dazzle—it's about a memorable experience. Frankly, that's a lot harder than opening up your wallet and buying fancy gadgets. That's not to say technology isn't important. But all the technology in the world can't cover up a bad experience.

FINDING MR. RIGHT

I'm still a relatively young guy, I guess, but every day I'm beginning to feel a little bit older. The hair product I wear in my hair helps cover it, but the grey is beginning to show through. When I play basketball with the guys at the gym, it takes me a day or two to recover. Many of those guys are much younger than I am. I can tell because they're the guys with "ink." I guess that's the vernacular the young people use these days to describe having tattoos. I must be getting older, because I don't have ink.

My daughter thinks I'm still hip, though, because I shop for jeans at The Buckle. It's only going to be a few more years, however, when she finally realizes that her dad's not "all that." (Just trying to talk like the young people.) She'll figure out that I'm just trying to act younger than I really am. The gig will probably be up when she finds out that cool people don't normally listen to smooth jazz. When my daughter realizes the shopping trips to The Buckle are just a big charade, that's probably when I'll officially become an old guy.

On the journey to becoming an old guy, here's what I've learned: who you have on your team really matters. In fact, I don't think it's an overstatement to suggest that it matters more than anything else when it comes to building a successful business or ministry. The team matters. You can have a solid mission and vision for the future. You can implement the best ministry strategy, systems, and structure. You can have really cool music—even better than smooth jazz. You can also be in God's Word daily, be fully empowered by the Spirit, and pray a lot. But if you don't have the right people on your team, you're not going to have success in what you do. Really. It's all that.

Building the best team, of course, begins before you hire your new staff member. It starts in the recruitment and selection process. It might be helpful to illustrate this by thinking about the days when you were young and your hormones were raging, when you were just beginning to figure out about relationships and love and dreaming about the prospects of marriage. There's a correlation between courting your future mate and the hiring process.

For example, you see some person who, on paper, has the right mix of skills and experience. He or she loves Jesus and is also available to fill the position that's vacant. You think—that's my prince charming or my fairy-tale princess. I want to marry that person. The problem is that you haven't found true love. You're just in lust with that person. Hiring someone just because they have the right education or the right job experience or the right skills is like marrying someone just because they look hot in jeans from The Buckle. Your eyes and your hormones tell you, "That's the one," when in reality you need more time for your head and your heart to confirm that the relationship will allow you to live happily ever after.

You need to go on lots of dates with this person, and you need to give yourself the freedom to date other people. Interview your prospective team members one-on-one. Have someone else interview them. Schedule group dates and invite a whole team of people to talk to the people you think may become "Mr. or Mrs. Right." Call their references and find out what they were like in previous jobs or relationships. You may even want them to take personality tests to see if their true colors match who they are when they're trying to impress you.

All of this dating before marriage hopefully ensures that you offer the ring to the right person. Just like a real marriage relationship, it's more likely to last because of the intangibles you discover over time rather than the details you might find on someone's resume during the first date. Forget about education, experience, and skills for a moment, and answer these questions:

- *Does this person love our church?* Have they demonstrated that they fully embrace our mission, vision, and values?
- *What motivates this person?* Will they soar in the role I have to offer, or will it become just a job to earn a paycheck?
- *Does he or she want to continue to grow?* Does she like to read? Does he take time to think? Does she make it a priority to dream and to create?
- *Is this person a leader?* With a limited amount of money to invest in staff, I need someone who will help me multiply the ministry. Will this person help me do that?
- *Does this person have a track record of success?* Do they have the potential to help the church reach the next level?
- *Do I like this person?* Does he or she have a fun personality? Am I going to enjoy spending fifty hours or more each week with this person?

In my experience, these questions are far more important when trying to find the best talent than learning whether or not someone has a big, fancy resume. Take this advice from a soon-to-be old guy without ink: don't marry the first hottie that comes along. I know what you're feeling. I've been there too. You have a vacant position and you're thinking, "We

TONY MORGAN

have people to reach for Jesus. I can't be doing my job and covering that open position at the same time. I need to hire her even though she may not be the best fit. My proverbial clock is ticking, and I'm not getting any younger, you know."

Just slow down, Mr. My-life-will-fall-apart-if-I-don't-hire-this-person-right-away. You will be far happier in the long run if you find someone who not only can do the job, but someone who will fit in well with the rest of the team and will add huge value to your ministry. That process takes time. It's better to leave a position vacant than to fill it with someone who's really not the best fit but just happens to be the best available.

I may not be the hippest guy in town, but hopefully I've helped you learn how to attract and select the very best talent for your team. And with the right pair of jeans, I think you could be all that.

FIXING THE MUSTANG

What you are about to read, as embarrassing as it may be, is a true story. None of the characters' names have been changed to protect the innocent . . . or the guilty. Every detail is authentic. Believe me. You can't make this stuff up.

A few years ago I took a vacation with Emily. We headed to the beach without the kids. Just us. Now I'm not a big spender, but I splurged a little on this vacation because it had been a long time since Emily and I had gone on a trip by ourselves. I rented a nice condo right on the beach. And I decided we would rent a fun car for the week as well.

It's true, isn't it? Doesn't the car make the man? The rental car agent offered me a Chevy Lumina, but I thought, "Hey, I'm on vacation with my wife. She's incredible. I'm madly in love with her. She's looking hot. I want her to think I'm hot too." Everyone knows Luminas aren't very sexy, so I decided to upgrade. I paid the extra to go with a brand new Mustang convertible.

It was a sweet ride. We really had a fun time with the car. We drove around with the top down most of the week. The car was fast. It was powerful. It was sleek. But most important of all, I think Emily thought I looked good behind the wheel.

Well, the night before we left, I did something that I don't normally do. Before I tell you, let me first explain that I'm not at all mechanical. In fact, Emily is much more mechanical than I am. Her dad is an engineer. He knows how to fix things. They say women tend to marry guys like their dads. That wasn't the case with Emily. She married someone who knows how to pick up the phone and hire someone to fix things.

So again, it's the last evening of our vacation. I don't know what possessed me to do this, but I decided I wanted to look under the hood of the Mustang. I'm not sure what I thought I was going to find under there. Remember, I'm not mechanical. And I certainly don't know anything about what's under the hood of a car. Well, I popped the hood. Opened it up. Confirmed that Mustangs do indeed have engines. And then I attempted to shut the hood.

I say "attempted," because that's when I began to run into problems. The hood wouldn't close. Apparently there are two latches. The first one was catching, but the second latch wasn't working properly. The hood wouldn't close all the way. I tried everything I could do to fix it but, remember, I'm not very mechanical.

So the next morning we headed back to the airport. The hood was still not completely closed, which wasn't a problem while we were driving through town. But once we hit the highway, the wind hit the front of the car, and that started the hood bouncing up and down. I didn't know what was going to happen. In addition to the embarrassment and noise, I was a little bit afraid that the pressure might break the first latch and send the hood flying back at us.

I knew this wasn't going to work for the fifty-mile trip to the airport. So the first chance I had, I got off the highway. I tried to find a garage to have someone try to fix the hood, but it was too early in the morning. Nothing was open except for a grocery store. And because I'm not very mechanical, I went into the grocery store to find the one thing I was positive would fix the hood of the car—duct tape. It took about four, twelve-inch strips of duct tape placed in precisely the right position to secure the hood of the car so we could finish the trip back to the airport.

Yes, I repaired the Mustang with duct tape. You can only imagine what the people at Hertz thought about my repair job when I returned the car. And regrettably, though I opted for the upgrade to the Mustang, Emily didn't think I was so hot after I demonstrated my lack of mechanical prowess.

Now I would not share this embarrassing story if I didn't think we could redeem it for a worthwhile purpose. But I think there are, in fact, a few helpful lessons we can learn from this experience. And if you'll indulge me for a moment, those lessons may even apply to your life and ministry. Here's what I learned:

- You can have the fastest car in the world, but if you don't have any idea what's under the hood, that can lead to trouble.
- The problem may not be an issue when you're cruising around town, but it will certainly be evident when you start to pick up speed.
- And you're only fooling yourself if you think a few well-placed strips of duct tape are going to fix your problem.

Churches of every size and shape face similar challenges. We try to encourage growth and health in our ministries, but if the right foundations aren't in place, it'll be difficult, if not impossible, to pick up speed. Then when growth happens, it'll magnify any foundational weaknesses that exist.

TONY MORGAN

Now as I said, I'm not very mechanical, but I do know how to ask questions. Whenever I have a problem with my car, I take it to my mechanic and I start asking questions to see what it will take to get me back on the road. That's also how I approach life and ministry. I'm constantly asking questions as I take steps in my faith and as I'm trying to fulfill my mission. Out of those questions I try to land on strategies—strategies that will hopefully allow us to reach people for Jesus. I'm also trying to encourage other churches. We need more growing, dynamic ministries that are having real impact in people's lives. That's our goal, isn't it? We're in the life-transformation business. We want to see people give up their lives filled with pain and anger and sorrow and exchange them for lives of love, hope, and purpose that can only be found through the transforming grace of Jesus Christ.

Now, nothing can replace God's presence and power in our ministry. We certainly need to remain in step with wherever he takes our churches. We can accomplish nothing apart from God. He builds the church, but we have to remember that he's called us to be builders. We are to be engaged in an active faith. God has given us a mission. And we have the Holy Spirit to guide us in our leadership. With that, I strongly believe that there are some challenging questions we need to ask—questions that can lead to strategic directions that allow our ministry to more effectively impact people's lives. In fact, I would argue that sometimes we may be asking "Do we have enough faith?" when we *should* be asking "What barriers do we need to remove for us to be more effective in our mission?"

What about you? Are you ready to put the duct tape back on the shelf?

A FOCUSED MESSAGE

I heard several folks comment on the movie *Spider-Man 3* when it premiered in theaters. Many of the reviews sounded like the one from my good friend Josh Griffin (more thandodgeball.com) out at Saddleback Church. Josh wrote:

"In short, I think they just tried to pack too much in one movie. Too many plot points, too many villains . . . too much of, well, everything. It was too long, and had more than enough story—yet in the end have we really come any further than when we started the movie?"[18]

Too much. Too many plot points. Too long. Too bad we make this same mistake with our stories and messages. We rarely leave our audience wanting more. It's a reminder that:

- A focused message makes for a better blog.
- A focused message makes for a better Web site.
- A focused message makes for a better service.
- A focused message makes for a better advertisement.
- A focused message makes for a better sermon.

The problem, of course, is that we get lazy. Focusing what we have to say is difficult. It takes more preparation. We have to go the extra step of honing our message. The great communicators, though, figure out how to share their message with as few words as possible.

When we focus our message, it becomes more memorable. It can be repeated more easily. It grabs attention and keeps it. And in the end, we have a better chance of moving people from point A to point B. Have we really come any further than when we started the movie? Maybe we should be asking that question more often.

FOLLOW THE LEADER

As if being a leader isn't tough enough, one day you wake up and realize: I can't do this by myself; I need to find others to help. This realization gets multiplied throughout the life of any growing and vibrant organization. Unless there's a commitment in place to identify, develop, and empower potential leaders, the scope of your impact and influence will always be limited. You may not feel it today, but at some point in the future the momentum will slow and the growth will begin to exceed your leadership capacity.

But it doesn't have to be that way. When you've built a church where new leadership is valued and embraced, the impact God can have through your ministry is greater than you could ever have imagined.

When ministry is sustained over time, it's because leadership is being multiplied. But to make it happen takes more than implementing a program. And it's not something you can experience in an instant. The multiplication of leadership is something that is nurtured over time. It involves a continuous focus that's mostly about cultivating an environment where leadership is welcomed and encouraged to grow. How do you cultivate that environment? You can begin by doing the following:

- *Communicate a big vision.* Remind people often. Then do it again. People want to know that they're giving their time and energy to something that really counts. Particularly with ministry, where leaders are usually volunteering their time, they need to know that they're investing in something of significance—something big. One of your primary roles as a leader is to always remind people of the mission God has called you to accomplish as a church. Without a compelling vision, you'll never attract high capacity leaders.

- *Point to the destination.* Let others determine how to get there. Your job is vision. You get to set expectations. We'll allow you to remind people of the values that should shape their decisions and actions. But when you begin to tell people specifically how to do it, they'll assume you don't need their leadership. These leaders need to own it. If you're just asking them to accomplish a task, they'll get it done for you, but then they'll find something else to do. Eric Schmidt, the CEO of Google, described it this way. "The most clever ideas don't come from the leaders, but rather from the leaders listening and encouraging and kind of creating a discussion. Wander around and try to find the new ideas."[19]

- *Find people who are smarter than you.* And give them the keys to the car. Leaders who don't have a chance to have an influence will take their influence elsewhere. Give people the freedom to succeed. Do everything you can to help them win. Again, you're not letting them drive anywhere they want. You get to identify the destination and help get them back on track if they get lost. You just always have to remember that leaders don't want to be passengers. They want to have the chance to drive.

- *Think relationships before you think results.* People, especially other leaders, need your time. They need to know who you are—your heart, your passions, your desires. And they need to know you care about them. That means you must invest your time with other key leaders and potential leaders and encourage them to do the same. This takes intentionality. You have to be committed to relationships. They don't just happen. As leaders, we tend to get focused on the task rather than the people. But in ministry especially, it's all about the people. Your leadership will only go as far as the relationships you've built . . . and no further.

As you're considering these thoughts on how to create an environment that fosters leadership development, consider what potential leaders are thinking. Here are some of the key questions people will be asking as they think about opportunities to step into leadership roles within your church:

- Am I needed? Is there a place for my gifts and skills?
- Will I have input? Will they listen to what I have to say?

- Will they keep me in the loop? Will I have information before others do?
- Do they care about me, or are they just using me?
- Will I have freedom to do my thing? Will they allow me to lead?
- Do I get to do something significant? Does this investment have a return?

You can't do it alone. It takes a team of empowered leaders to take ministry to the next level. What are you doing to multiply and release the leadership potential in your church? And are you creating an environment where high-capacity leaders are welcomed and challenged to be all that God created them to be? That may be your biggest challenge as a leader.

FOX NEWS CALLED

I got a call at the house today from FOX News, wanting me to do an interview on "FOX & Friends" in the morning. Though I really wanted to talk to them and to be on television, I thought it was probably more appropriate that the senior pastor handle this one. So I declined. I can tell all my friends now that I turned down an interview with FOX News. Love that.

I found out later this afternoon that they called a few of the other pastors before me, which once again proves that I'm not "all that." I just happen to be the only pastor without a life who was at home on a Saturday afternoon to answer my phone. But I don't care. I'm still telling my friends that FOX News wanted to talk to me.

It's a good reminder that we should always be prepared when the media calls. Don't be fooled. They don't always report news; they're often also creating the news. And many times they're willing to talk to the *available* person rather than the *knowledgeable* person to develop their story.

FRESH BREATH

Today I live in Anderson, South Carolina, but I grew up in Piqua, Ohio. Since I once lived in Piqua, that means I used to be a Piquad (pronounced "pick-wad"). That's what they call people who live in Piqua. As if redneck jokes aren't enough, now you can start telling jokes about the guy you know who used to be a Piquad.

This coming weekend I'll be hanging out, as usual, at NewSpring. If I was traveling back home to Ohio, though, I'd consider visiting Crossroads Community Church (cross roads.net). Crossroads understands the power of packaging a series. Take, for example, a series of messages on prayer called "Fresh Breath." According to Brian Tome, the senior pastor, "Prayer should be as easy, natural, and spontaneous as breathing." He used this series to creatively teach on a core spiritual discipline.[20]

Crossroads makes all their messages available through an online message archive on their Web site. You may also want to check out CrazyChurch.com. Through that site, Crossroads is partnering with three other churches to provide creative ministry resources for FREE. Now that's a cool idea! It may not be as cool as being a Piquad, but it's still pretty darn cool.

THE GAME WON'T COME TO YOU

When the weather gets colder, I begin to shift my attention from golf to basketball. And for the last several weeks, I've been heading to the gym with my neighbor Lou to play some pick-up basketball. Lou knows basketball. He used to coach at the college level. Then kids came along and his focus changed. I can certainly relate.

Since Lou knows basketball, I'm not sure why he called me a month ago to be included in his regular Tuesday night game. Week after week I've been going with Lou and getting schooled on the court. Just about every player is younger, faster, stronger, and jumps higher. Come to find out from Lou, a number of these guys also played college ball. I'm in way over my head.

I'm probably a better than average shooter. But that's my entire game. I stand and shoot. Sometimes when I'm really aggressive, I take one dribble to the left and *then* I shoot. I've learned, however, that my stand-and-shoot game doesn't work with these guys. They know how to move on the court. They know how to get open and create scoring opportunities. I wish I had game like those guys.

So as I suggested, I'm not exactly sure why Lou called me. But I'm beginning to draw some conclusions. In fact, I can probably think of at least:

✦ ✦ 10 GOOD REASONS LOU PICKED ✦ ✦
TONY MORGAN FOR HIS TEAM

1. He knows how to color coordinate his gym shorts with his t-shirt.
2. He doesn't hog the ball because he can't *get* the ball.
3. He doesn't sweat as much as the average player.
4. He has good health insurance for when he gets hurt.
5. He can count to eleven by ones and twos, so he can keep score.
6. He's not inclined to slap other guys' butts after each bucket.
7. He's a lean, mean, pass-the-ball-to-guys-that-know-how-to-play-the-game machine.
8. He has a decent job, so he could afford the $25.00 for court rental.
9. He makes everyone else on the court look good.
10. He's Lou's neighbor.

My stand-and-shoot game doesn't work with these guys. As the level of play increases, the game gets faster and more physical. You quickly learn that you can't stand around and let the game come to you. The best players at this level know how to move with and without the ball. They're called "playmakers." They generate scoring opportunities.

Ministry isn't much different. You can't just sit around and wait for the game to come to you. Yes, God's moving and, yes, we need to keep praying for his wisdom and direction.

However, we can't just sit on our hands and wait for God to do something. He's called us to be a part of his mission. I've learned time after time that God reveals his plans as I begin to take steps of obedience.

Remember what God told Joshua before the Israelites crossed the Jordan River? God instructed Joshua to relay to the priests that they were to "go and stand in the river" (Josh. 3:8). If I'm a priest, I'm thinking that idea's all wet. However, they came up to the river and took that first step into the water. Remember what happened next? God moved and the water stopped flowing. The nation of Israel crossed the Jordan. It all happened because they were obedient to God's command and took that first step.

So where are you today? Are you waiting for the game to come to you? I hope not. It's time to listen to the voice of God and do what he tells you to do. He wants you in the game. Do you know the next play? You better figure it out, because he'll stop passing you the ball if you don't know how to score.

GIANT INFLATABLE BLUE MONKEYS

As I was driving back and forth to the soccer field, this thought ran through my mind. At what point do you determine that your product or service just isn't attracting enough attention on its own and decide you have to bring in the giant inflatable blue monkey?

Does the management team sit around the conference room and talk about what it might take to improve the customer experience or improve the quality of the product or possibly adjust pricing strategies first? Do they run through all those scenarios and decide it's just easier and cheaper to rent the giant inflatable blue monkey?

What about you? Are you resorting to the "giant inflatable blue monkey" in your business or organization?

GOD'S WILL?

Back in late 2006, my wife and I were trying to decide whether or not we should move our family. It was a really huge decision. We were considering leaving more than eight years of friendships and ministry in Indiana to move to South Carolina to be a part of the ministry team at NewSpring.

As you might imagine, this decision was a major focus of our conversations for a number of weeks. Andy Stanley would suggest we need to approach decisions like this by answering the question, "What's the wise thing to do?" In his book *The Best Question Ever*, he said we need to ask this question in light of our past experiences, our present circumstances, and our future hopes and dreams.

With that in mind, our conversations centered around these key decision points:

1. *Vision*—Does NewSpring's vision make our hearts beat fast? Is their vision something we can embrace? Can we champion it?
2. *People*—Can we see ourselves on the team? Do they know how to have fun? Will they stretch us in our spiritual and leadership journeys? Will we be able to do the same for them?
3. *Place*—Can we see ourselves living in Anderson, South Carolina? Is it a place the Morgan family can call home? Can we see our kids growing up at NewSpring?
4. *Role*—Given my strengths, passions, and personality, does this role help me fulfill the call God has placed on my life? Will I be fulfilled? Will I be challenged? Will it be rewarding?

Obviously there were lots of other decision factors involved, but I thought it might be helpful for you to see the big topics that shaped our conversations. With the opportunity for a big adventure in front of us, we talked with friends, we talked with family, and we talked with God. By the end of our process, the encouragement to pursue this opportunity seemed to be almost unanimous.

To be honest, neither Emily nor I heard God audibly talk to us. That kind of stuff hasn't happened to me. I'm confident, though, that God talks to us through his Word and through the counsel of others. And as a result, Emily and I determined this is what God wanted us to do next. We determined it was the wise thing to do.

GOING SOCIAL

When USATODAY.com relaunched with a new look in 2007, the primary objective was to create methods for interaction and conversation on their site. In other words, their site isn't just about news stories for us to read. They're also trying to engage us in a dialogue. They know we don't just digest the news anymore. Sometimes we also discover and generate the news. Here are some features of their Web site:

- Readers can write a comment on every story.
- You can create a free profile with information about yourself, your photo, and the ability to start a blog.
- *USA Today* journalists are also participating in the online community by creating profiles, joining you in conversation and asking for thoughts and experiences around different stories.

- Every story lets you vote for it, bumping it up a most-recommended list.
- You can click bylines and instantly find more articles by that reporter.
- The homepage will feature lists of most-read, most-sent, most-commented, and most-recommended stories.
- They're providing live news feeds and linking you straight to the sites of competing news sources.
- They're encouraging readers to upload photos around different stories and events.[21]

It might be a fun exercise for your team to run through this list of new features on the USATODAY.com site and ask yourselves, "Does the Web site for our organization engage conversation and help connect people into community, or are we just spewing information about who we are and what we do?"

You have to help people experience who you are and interact with your organization. If you're just giving people pretty pictures and sharing information on your Web site like it's an online service bulletin, they're probably not using your Web site. Sorry to break that news to you. Better that *I* share it, though, than you read about it on the front page of the *USA Today*.

GOOGLE AND THE ART OF STRATEGY

I read a great *Wired* magazine interview with Eric Schmidt, the CEO of one of my favorite companies, Google. Here are

three excerpts that should challenge our thinking about the future of ministry:

Google on Video

"We really do think the YouTube phenomenon is a sustainable one for many, many years. And the argument is very simple: People are using video everywhere. People are building communities of people who use video. They're sharing them. YouTube's traffic continues to grow very quickly. Video is something we think is going to be embedded everywhere. And it makes sense, from Google's perspective, to be the operator of the largest site that contains all that video."[22]

- How are you incorporating video into your weekend services? In my opinion (and they don't pay me to say this anymore), nobody does this better than Granger Community Church (gccwired.com). Check the media player on their Web site.
- How are you using video to share your service experience on the Web?
- Are you prepared to engage online conversations by bringing a biblical influence to existing social networks using video technology?

Google on Systems Standardization

"The information systems within the company are quite good. But we've reined in certain things. For example, we don't tolerate the kind of 'Hey, I want to have my own database and have a good time' behavior that was very effective for us five years ago. The cost of this from a manageability, maintenance, and scaling perspective has become a problem. So virtually all of the product groups are now told, 'Build on top of this common set of services.' That means internally we now use exactly the same code running on the same servers—like Gmail and Calendar and Google apps—as our customers do."

- How many different databases (think ministry mailing lists) exist within your ministry? If it's more than one, it's too many.
- Are you paying attention to the strength of your infrastructure (computer network, database solutions, Web solutions, communications solutions, etc.) and standardizing and enhancing these areas to create synergy for ministry impact?

Google on Idea Implementation

"Fast learners win. We're in new, uncharted space. So the traditional assumptions that you and I might have about the future might actually just be wrong. There might be a new answer. And the only way to discover that is to put out your idea and then test it. And we track the results of that very, very, very rigorously, and this is not something we talk a lot about, but it's critical for us. How are these new ideas doing? What's their growth rate? What are the issues around them? And we push. What can we do to accelerate the development of this feature? What's the new problem? What's the new opportunity?"

TONY MORGAN

- What are you doing within your culture to encourage new ideas without allowing mission drift?
- How quickly do new ideas get implemented? Does your decision-making model allow for rapid deployment and testing, or do ideas get bogged down in meeting discussions?
- Does your ministry environment encourage ideas that periodically fail?

GUNKY BUILD-UP

I saw this sign at a gas station while I was traveling. It made me think about instances when I've had to deal with gunky build-up in my life. For me, gunky build-up occurs when I let less important stuff squeeze out the real priorities in my life. Maybe you've experienced this too.

- Sometimes I believe the lie that I can't afford to take a break and rest. The reality is that I'm far less effective in my family and leadership roles when I'm tired and grumpy.
- Sometimes I believe the lie that I'll spend quality time with my wife at the end of the day after everything else is done. The reality is that the last things on my priority list rarely get done.
- Sometimes I believe the lie that I'll get to the next big projects after I knock out the more routine tasks. The reality is that there will always be other routine tasks to complete.

KILLING COCKROACHES

- Sometimes I believe the lie that the more I do, the more valuable I am to the team. The reality is that I'm not being effective if I'm busy doing the wrong things.
- Sometimes I believe the lie that the little problem I have isn't jeopardizing my leadership. The reality is that most times everyone else is already being impacted by my little problem.
- Sometimes I believe the lie that I need to correct every false statement and negative comment. The reality is that many times those faint voices become a distraction when I draw attention and make them loud.

TONY MORGAN

- Sometimes I believe the lie that goals will be accomplished without a plan if I'm just patient and faithful. The reality is that most goals worth pursuing require counsel and strategy and hard work and commitment.
- Sometimes I believe the lie that I need to jump at a good opportunity. The reality is that someone will always have a good opportunity for me to pursue, and many times those good opportunities squeeze out time and energy needed to fulfill a greater mission and calling.

Do you know what I'm talking about? Have you dealt with similar cases of gunky build-up? I'm still trying to learn how to deal with this, but along the way I've also learned some preventive maintenance that helps clean up my engine. Here are some things I've learned I need to do to "de-gunk" my life:

- Schedule my week in advance, including scheduling time to work on major projects.
- Prioritize time with my wife.
- Surround myself with friends who will push back when needed.
- Stay disciplined about my faith, my exercise, and my eating habits.
- Learn to say no.
- Decide in advance what I hope to accomplish.

I've also seen gunk show up in ministries and other organizations. Sometimes, for example, gunk comes in the form of ministry programming and events. Good programs get added on and added on to the point that they squeeze out what's most effective in helping people take steps in their faith. Or worse yet, ministry programming and events become so numerous that they start competing against each other. Gunk is bad for people, but it's also bad for churches.

So is it time for you to stop the gunky build-up in your life or in your ministry? Now is the time to do something about it. Don't delay. And don't let yourself get in a funk because you're unwilling to deal with your gunk.

GUY KAWASAKI
FIVE QUESTIONS

BACKSTORY—Guy first made a name for himself at Apple Computer, where he was part of a team that was responsible for marketing the Macintosh com- puter. He's a Silicon Valley venture capitalist noted for bringing the concept of evangelism to high-tech business. He is currently CEO of Garage Technology Ventures, a venture capital firm that specializes in high-tech startups located in Silicon Valley, California. More importantly, he frequently shares his thoughts on his blog (blog.guykawasaki.com). Excerpts from my e-mail interview with him:

TONY: I don't ever want to be considered a "bozo." What's your best advice for avoiding bozo-osity?
GUY: Give them one good shot. If they don't get it, then move on. Life, even eternal life, is too short.

Honestly, I know this is true in business. It might not be so true in your business.

TONY: What's a recent learning that has rocked your world?

GUY: Nothing too radical here. I learned how much I love my kids, if that counts.

TONY: I don't own an Apple computer. I feel like I'm missing out. Am I?

GUY: This is like me asking you, "I don't believe in God. Am I missing out?"

TONY: I have friends who stand up in pulpits every weekend and teach. Can you help them by explaining your 10/20/30 rules of PowerPoint?

GUY: The crux is that a PowerPoint user should use ten slides in twenty minutes and use a large (30 point) font. Now most ministers don't use PowerPoint, but the message is the same: keep it short and sweet.

TONY: You call yourself an evangelist. In your mind, what makes a good evangelist?

GUY: 90 percent is having a good cause. It's very easy to evangelize a good cause. It's hard to evangelize [junk].

HALLOWEEN

I probably shouldn't admit this, but I love Halloween. As a Christian, I know, I'm not supposed to love Halloween, but I do. Here's why:

- Friends from my neighborhood come to my front door unannounced to visit.
- I get to meet neighbors I haven't met before.
- I have the opportunity to engage in conversations I would not normally have.
- My kids are darn cute when they dress up in costumes.
- My home feels warm and inviting after being outside for a couple of hours.
- No one is expecting me to do anything "pastoral" on Halloween evening. I can just be normal Tony.
- I have a rich assortment of candy that I can steal from my kids.
- I get to enjoy a fun evening with my family.

I'm probably going to get slammed for admitting this. After all, Halloween is supposed to be the evil holiday. But until someone comes up with an alternative holiday where I get to connect with my neighbors and enjoy quality family time, I'm going to be a fan of Halloween.

Just in case you're wondering, I'm also a fan of MySpace and Facebook and Twitter. Yes, they can used for evil too. But rather than climbing into an Internet cocoon with other Christ followers, what would happen if we decided to engage the conversations already taking place on these social networking sites? It's amazing to me how God can redeem something in culture to open spiritual conversations with people who are far from Christ. Wouldn't it be something if Christ followers embraced these opportunities rather than trying to create a Christian alternative to every cultural fad? We might actually

TONY MORGAN

begin to offer positive influence to a world that desperately needs Jesus.

HEAVEN

I sat down by Howard at our staff meeting this morning. Howard was drinking a cup of Starbucks coffee imported from Greenville. Howard may go to "the hot place" for bringing his Starbucks coffee into Anderson, South Carolina—the land of Starbucksless Coffeedom. Howard works for me, but not for long if he continues sauntering through the office while brandishing his imported coffee.

That aside, the quote on Howard's coffee cup caught my attention this morning. Here it is: "The Way I See It." #230.

"Heaven is totally overrated. It seems boring. Clouds, listening to people play the harp. It should be somewhere you can't wait to go, like a luxury hotel. Maybe blue skies and soft music were enough to keep people in line in the 17th century, but heaven has to step it up a bit. They're basically getting by because they only have to be better than hell."—Joel Stein, columnist for the *Los Angeles Times*

So here's the deal. There is nothing in the Bible, of course, to support Stein's understanding of heaven. And because of that, I guess we could be angry with Mr. Stein for flippantly making this quote without researching the facts. Or we could slam the *LA Times* for employing someone who so carelessly attacks people of faith. Or we could boycott Starbucks because they're promoting an anti-God agenda. Personally, I couldn't care less about all of that.

Do you know what angers me about this quote? This is an indictment of the church! We've let the greatest message in the world become "clouds" and "people playing harps." We're known more for yelling at people and telling them they're going to hell than we are for trying to help people find hope and purpose. We've let the media neuter the most dangerous message ever told. That's what makes me angry about that coffee cup.

To be honest, I'm thankful Starbucks has generated this conversation. The church needs to wake up. We may be communicating the truth, but people aren't listening. That's not a message problem—that's a method problem.

HIRING THE RIGHT LEADER

Someone asked me recently about the leaders we hire in our organization. I may not share the exact same view on this as the other pastors I work with, but I thought you might be interested in my response.

Let me say this right up front: the reason the leaders on my team are so successful in their roles is because they first love Jesus. In a very close second, they also love our ministry. I believe that's the key to any successful ministry hire, especially in a leadership role. The person has to love the church.

And that's why we typically try to hire people from the inside—people who already attend and serve at our church. We already know the stuff that's hard to measure because we've had a chance to witness their faith journey. We've seen how they interact with others. We know their passion for what they do and their heart for the ministry. Frankly, I think it's all these variables that don't show up on a resumé that really determine the success of someone's role on the team.

Regarding skills, there are probably some basic skills and experiences that are required for any position. You probably know these better than I do. Here's why I hire the leaders I hire. I don't hire them to do the role. I hire them to:

- Champion the mission, vision, and values of our church.
- Build teams with staff and, primarily, with volunteers.
- Manage significant projects.
- Model loyalty to the pastoral leadership team.
- Bring the right resources to the right projects.
- Think strategically about systems, especially as these relate to helping people connect to our ministry.
- Learn what the best marketplace leaders are doing and help us implement similar strategies to reach people for Jesus Christ.
- Help us operate and get our message out as if we're a church of 16,000 rather than a church of 8,000.

And, this may just be me, but I love working with leaders who are confident about who they are and what they *need* to do, yet they are humble about who they are and what they *get* to do. I'm looking for that perfect balance. The leaders I work with need to have the confidence to push back when they don't agree with a direction we're taking. That's a good thing. But by the same token, I need to have complete confidence that he or she trusts the leadership. Even in instances where there's disagreement (hopefully that's rare), the leaders on my team will be in the trenches championing where we're going next. Again, that's a part of someone's character that doesn't show up on a resumé.

What do you think? Am I hiring the right leaders? What am I missing?

HOW WOULD APPLE DO CHURCH?

I had a fun brainstorming session recently with my team. Now you can play along. Remember, this is brainstorming. There are no wrong answers.

Let's pretend a company like Apple was committed to reaching people for Jesus. Obviously they're trying to reach the same people we're trying to reach. The only difference is that instead of selling iPods and Macs and iPhones, we're presenting the gospel. It's a stretch, I know. But we're trying to discover new ministry strategies to reach people in today's culture. So here's the question to brainstorm: If Apple was a church, how would Apple do church?

Then when you're done with that, try substituting some other companies that are taking new ground in today's culture like Google or Starbucks or Target or Facebook.

How would you answer the question?

I'M JUST NOT THAT INTERESTED IN GOD

Just in case you've forgotten that not everyone thinks or believes like you, check out this quote: "I'm not religious.

TONY MORGAN

I don't think much about God, except when I am in a pinch and need some special favors. I have no particular reason to think he'll deliver, but I sometimes take a shot anyway. Other than that, I'm just not that interested in God."[23]

This quote comes from Steven Levitt's blog post on *The New York Times* Web site. Levitt is one of the authors of *Freakonomics,* which, by the way, is a great book.

I'm fascinated that Levitt would be vulnerable like this with his thoughts about God and religion. Not many people have the courage to offer statements like that. Based on what he said, we know:

- He's not looking for religion. (And I don't blame him.)
- Though he doesn't have a relationship with God, his comments suggest he believes there *is* a God.
- There are times when Levitt practices the discipline of prayer even when he doesn't have faith that those prayers will be answered.

I wonder how many more people there are like Levitt. I'm guessing there are a bunch. What would happen if there was a church that didn't attack people like him but rather designed their ministries to help nonreligious people connect with God, especially in those times when folks are "in a pinch"?

It's possible someone like Levitt may never experience what a healthy relationship with Jesus looks like. But rather than attacking guys like him, I'd sure like to pour my life into creating a church that tries to minister to guys like him.

IMPOSSIBLE RELIGIOUS DEMANDS

Jesus said, "How terrible it will be for you experts in religious law! For you crush people beneath impossible religious demands, and you never lift a finger to help ease the burden" (Luke 11:46 NLT).

Do you think Jesus was just addressing the "law versus grace" issue, or do you think this same teaching applies to what we're asking people to do in our ministries today? As we ask people to commit to spiritual disciplines, attend services, participate in events, serve in ministry, connect in groups, reach out to people in need, and build relationships with those outside the church—all of which can be helpful in our spiritual growth—are we creating "impossible religious demands"? What's our responsibility to "ease the burden" in people's lives? Is that part of our responsibility as ministry leaders?

INFORMATION OR VISION

I'm surrounded by great leaders who are much smarter than I am. They're constantly challenging me, and it's pushing me to grow in my leadership. Like today: I'm sitting in a meeting talking with my teammates about what we do (and don't) communicate, when Shane (shaneduffey.com) steps to the plate with this statement: "People will follow vision. They won't follow information."

We sometimes think that if we just give people more information, they'll naturally be more likely to connect and engage in ministry. More often than not, however, more

TONY MORGAN

information creates more confusion over what's really important. It's distracting. It's overwhelming. People stop listening.

People do follow vision, however. In fact, they're energized and unified by it. If it's a God-ordained vision and the right leadership team stewards that vision well, it can have the power to transform people's lives.

INVEST AND INVITE

The other day I had a conversation with my longtime friend "Ted." He and I regularly get together for lunch two or three times a month. Ted's a good guy, a family man. Sometimes he goes to church, but he hasn't committed his life to Jesus Christ.

You need to know that my evangelistic style is very relational. I need to invest in a relationship—sometimes for months—before I invite someone to take his or her next step toward Christ. It takes time to develop that kind of trust.

Over lunch I invited Ted to join me for a worship service. I'm convinced that if he'd go just one time, he'd love the experience. Ted's a bit of a rocker, so I think he'd really love the music. And I would really love for him to hear about how Jesus could transform his life.

Admittedly a conversation like this can be awkward, but I very much enjoyed inviting Ted to church. You know why? My church has made it easy for regular attendees to invite unbelievers to church. Your church can use the same strategies we do. Here are four proven ways to help attendees invest and invite:

- *Plan your services and let members know in advance what's coming.* It's much easier to invite someone to church when you know what the pastor will be talking about.
- *Use culturally hot topics to address relevant, biblical teachings.* This makes it easy for members to talk with their friends about the service.
- *Prepare postcards with details about the upcoming series:* dates, times, children's ministry information, and directions. Members then have a printed piece in hand that can be used as an invitation.
- *Intentionally create a service that will be welcoming and compelling for newcomers.* Make sure members never have to wonder if their friends will feel uncomfortable. They may be challenged, but they'll never be embarrassed.

I'm not able to wrap my story up in a tidy little package. Ted declined my invitation. But the invite to a new series started a great conversation about Jesus. Ted had lots of questions about whether or not Jesus was who he and others said he was. He was asking the types of questions that gave me hope that one day, hopefully soon, Ted will commit his life to Christ. Until then, I'll continue to invest and invite.[24]

IRRELEVANT

The guys over at ChurchMarketingSucks.com completed an online poll confirming that 78 percent of respondents didn't think their church Web site was worth bragging about.[25] In a day when we rely so heavily on the Web to gather information, make decisions, and interact with each other, this should be alarming. I remember when it was music style that used to make the church look dated and irrelevant.

JESUS IN A BOX

We've been praying for this moment for quite some time. Emily found Jesus. She was a seeker. She knew there was something missing in her life. Fortunately she found him.

Turns out, he was under the couch in our family room the entire time. In the process of preparing for our move to South Carolina, we were having the carpets cleaned. When we pulled the couch out of the family room, there he was. You see, we'd been missing the little, rubber, infant Jesus that goes with the kids' nativity set. We thought we'd left him in the condo we stayed in during vacation. Turns out he was under the couch the entire time. Once we found him, we put Jesus in the storage area with the rest of our Christmas items, ready to be boxed up and shipped to South Carolina.

There's a bit of irony in that statement, isn't there? *Jesus in a box.* I think we sometimes tend to do that with the real Jesus as well. Think about it:

- Doesn't it seem like a lot of us live out our faith as though Jesus only exists in a building we visit on Sunday?
- Do you get the sense we sometimes like to worship our rules and practices more than God himself?

- Have we moved to a place where we think people will only accept Christ through a three-point message, a reflective song, and an invitation from the pastor?
- Have we lost how big God is by thinking he can't use talking donkeys and the bellies of a fish and burning bushes to get our attention today?

It's one thing when we put the little, rubber, nativity Jesus into a box. It's a completely different thing when we put the all-powerful, all-knowing creator of the universe in a box. We sometimes tend to do that.

Wonder what life and ministry would look like if we removed the box. More importantly, I wonder what miracles we've missed because we didn't realize Jesus has never been in the box.

I'm glad Emily found Jesus.

KATHY SIERRA
FIVE QUESTIONS

BACKSTORY—Kathy Sierra has been interested in the brain and artificial intelligence since her days as a game developer (Virgin, Amblin', MGM). She is the co-creator of the best-selling *Head First* series (named to Amazon's Top Ten Editor's Choice Computer Books for 2003 and 2004). She used to write for Creating Passionate Users (headrush.typepad.com), one of my favorite blogs.

TONY MORGAN

TONY: Has anyone told you that you draw great pictures on your blog? Why do the pictures capture my attention?

KATHY: Brains have been getting information from visuals for way longer than they've been processing words—pictures usually *are* worth a thousand words. Our brains are tuned to pay attention to images. After all, a change in light and shadow might be a tiger!

TONY: What's a recent learning that has rocked your world?

KATHY: Most of us know from experience that being around people with a strong emotion has an influence on our own emotions, but scientists have only recently begun to understand why. The discovery of "mirror neurons" shows that our brains are wired to mimic others around us, and the phenomenon of "emotional contagion" (where an angry person can spark anger in those around him, with anger propagating like a virus throughout a group) is extremely difficult to resist.

Your mother might have told you to have good role models or to stay away from someone who was a "bad influence," and now the neuroscientists are backing her up. In my own world, that means being more aware and careful to not get caught up when I'm around those who are bitter, cynical, chronically angry, etc., and choosing to spend more time around those who have the kind of outlook I want to have—optimistic, enthusiastic, and caring.

TONY: What's your favorite blog?

KATHY: I can't give you just one. But the most consistently helpful for me are 43 Folders (43folders.com), 37 Signals (37signals.com/svn), and Seth's blog (seth godin.typepad.com).

TONY: Churches are historically known for risk aversion. How do you challenge those who are afraid of change? Or is innovation overrated?

KATHY: A quote I heard once is that people aren't necessarily afraid of change. They're afraid of *being* changed. And the only way to help overcome that out-of-my-control feeling is to be proactive, to innovate and initiate change. Alan Kay, one of the earliest inventors of the graphical user interface, said, "The best way to predict the future is to invent it." When I meet with people who resist change, I try to help them work on creativity and the ability to both learn and unlearn as quickly as possible. The rate of change keeps increasing, and the future is not optional.

TONY: Why do people become passionate about using a product or service? How do we help people maintain that passion?

KATHY: When you look at things people are truly passionate about, you always find learning and growth and improvement. We're always trying to gain more knowledge and skill around the thing we're passionate about, because being better *is* better! When we're better at something, our experiences become richer, deeper, and more rewarding when we have the knowledge and skill to meet a challenge we believe is meaningful, whether it's playing great golf, listening to (and appreciating) classical music, or becoming involved in a cause we care about. To answer your first question, people become passionate about a product or service because that product or service (or the company who provides it) helps them get *really good* at something so they can have that richer, more meaningful experience.

We can help people maintain that passion by continuing to help them grow, offering new challenges and opportunities to acquire more knowledge and skill and experience. Also, people with a passion want to connect with others who share that passion, so anything we can do to support and encourage "affinity groups" is a tremendous help. People who feel more alone in their passion are often those who don't have anyone to share it with. Another thing we can do is help them find ways to introduce other people in their life to the thing they're passionate about. They *want* to evangelize, but they don't always have the tools. The most important people in their lives are the ones they most want to "get" why they have this passion.

KIDS SAY THE D$%&EST THINGS

Last evening we were sitting at the dinner table having a great family conversation. And as frequently happens, a question came up about a unique word that the kids had not heard before. When that happens at our house, someone runs into the living room and pulls the dictionary from the shelf and, together, we discover a new word.

Well, I mentioned that I was looking for a "D-word" and immediately Jacob, my eight-year-old son, started cracking up. He thought it was funny that his dad, a pastor, was looking up what in his mind was *the* "D-word." When I clarified for him that I was looking up a word that started with "D"—not *the* D-word—he said, "That's funny because I could have told you how to spell D$%&."

I must admit. It took everything I had to keep from laughing. I restrained myself, however, and kept my composure. And like all good fathers would, I asked Jacob where he learned that particular D-word. Did you learn it at school? Did you learn it on the bus? Did you learn it from one of your friends in the neighborhood? At which point Jacob explained that he learned that D-word from "the confetti over by the baseball diamond."

Of course I'm thinking, "Confetti by the baseball diamond? When have they had confetti at the baseball diamond? D$%& is such a short word—how did they get it on confetti?"

Stunned. Silent. Only for a moment. Then it registered. He meant *graffiti* by the baseball diamond.

There are things in our environment we grow immune to over time. Sometimes they appear to be innocuous like stains on ceiling tiles. We notice them at first, but then over time they become invisible to us. Just in case you forgot, hopefully this story about my son's experience at the ballpark reminds you that the environment really does matter. Whether you notice it or not, it's impacting people—especially those who are new on the scene.

When was the last time you shared the experience at your church with someone who had fresh eyes? When was the last time someone new shared their thoughts on your facility, your service, your guest experience, and the language you use in your communications. If you've been around for some time, it's invisible. You need those fresh eyes. They notice the stains and the graffiti.

KILLED BY NINJAS?

A friend came home from vacation with this picture:

They say "beggars can't be choosers," but I think this guy proved them wrong. Rather than pitch the same message that others have used before, he chose to be a little bit creative.

He distinguished himself from the crowd and tossed in a bit of humor. I'm guessing he gets better results than others on this same corner. He may not really be looking for karate lessons, but he just taught us a lesson in communications. That makes him a ninja in my book.

LEADERS

I've been watching people a lot recently. In person. On television. Looking for signs of leadership.

You need to know that I'm surrounded by great leaders. Because of that, I know what leadership looks like. You also need to know I fall into the group that happens to believe that God has *gifted* some to be leaders. Which means some have gifts that don't include leadership. That's a good thing. We need a great mix of gifts to have an impact in ministry or in any organization. It would be bad if we only had leaders.

As I've been watching for leaders to emerge during these last few weeks, I've noticed that there are several types of people. Some are genuine leaders. Some are in leadership positions but they aren't really leaders. Some aren't in a leadership position but think they should be. All of this has got me thinking about leadership and, well, signs that indicate you're not really a leader. Here are:

✦ ✦ 10 EASY WAYS TO KNOW ✦ ✦ YOU'RE NOT A LEADER

1. You're waiting on a bigger staff and more money to accomplish your vision.

TONY MORGAN

2. You think you need to be in charge in order to have influence.
3. You're content.
4. You tend to foster division instead of generating a helpful dialogue.
5. You think you need to say something to be heard.
6. You find it easier to blame others for your circumstances than to take responsibility for solutions.
7. It's been some time since you said, "I messed up."
8. You're driven by the task instead of the relationships and the vision.
9. Your dreams are so small that people think they can be achieved.
10. No one is following you.

There are probably others you can add to this list. Maybe you can help me do that. Let's be on the lookout for leaders. What sets them apart?

LEADERSHIP LESSONS I LEARNED FROM FOOTBALL

I went with two of my kids to our first Clemson football game recently. Clemson won. It was a great night. The kids had a blast. Here are five lessons I learned from the evening.

1. *If thousands of people make some noise, it can get pretty loud.* Jacob agreed that "Death Valley" is the loudest stadium we've ever been in. Don't know if that's because of the way it was constructed or just

because Clemson fans know how to get loud. When lots of people get focused on one thing, though, they can sure make some noise.

2. *People will do some crazy things to worship something they love.* Paint their bodies. Raise their arms. Jump around. Sing songs. Clap. Chant. Even in the craziness of a nationally televised game, though, there are security personnel who are charged with keeping the "worship" orderly. (It was really funny watching the students charge the field three different times at the end of the game.)

3. *When you really believe in something, you'll take a stand.* Clemson fans don't sit down. I haven't figured out why they installed seats in the stadium. The fans were on their feet for the entire four hours.

4. *People will put their money where their heart is.* They'll spend $30,000, as an example, just to own a piece of land to tailgate before and after the game. They'll invest millions of dollars into a facility to help recruit new athletes. It's amazing the cash people will lay down for something they love.

5. *When the cause is big enough, people will give their time.* I'm convinced time is our scarcest commodity today. But people started showing up very early the morning of the game to stake out their territory. They hung out with friends. They served each other meals. They walked miles to find parking spaces. They stood in the football stadium for more than four hours. They sat in traffic for a couple more hours after the game.

It takes a big investment of time to support something that's bigger than yourself.

LOADING PEOPLE DOWN

We had an interesting conversation on the golf course yesterday about ministry. It fed something in me that I've been thinking about for several years now. I keep going back to the Gospels and seeing how Jesus ripped apart the religious leaders for the burdens they were putting on people. At one point in Luke, for example, Jesus said to the religious leaders, "Woe to you, because you load people down with burdens they can hardly carry, and you yourselves will not lift one finger to help them," (Luke 11:46). Being a ministry leader myself, warnings like that catch my attention.

One of the volunteer leaders yesterday was pretty much admitting, "I'm burnt out. I'm tired. I need time to myself. I need a break." Obviously when I hear that, I'm not only concerned for the individual involved but as a ministry leader, it sends up a red flag. I wonder, "Am I really helping people take their next step toward Christ, or am I just loading them down with burdens?"

This may be the ultimate challenge I face in ministry. On the one hand, I want to "prepare God's people for works of service, so that the body of Christ may be built up" (Eph. 4:12), but on the other hand I want people to have a life-transforming relationship with Jesus who said: "Come to me, all you who are weary and burdened, and I will give you rest. Take my yoke upon you and learn from me, for I am gentle and humble in heart, and you will find rest for your souls. For my yoke is easy and my burden is light" (Matt. 11:28–30).

This raises conflict in my mind because it feels like the church (the local church in general) needs to create opportunities for people to experience Bible teaching, Bible study, serving opportunities, relational connections with fellow Christ followers, corporate worship, etc., so that people can jump on a discipleship track and take steps in their faith journey. But on the other hand, every time we ask people to take another step, we may also be doing the following:

- Adding to the already overwhelming pace of people's lives.
- Increasing the demand on volunteer ministry leaders who are also investing their precious time to serve others.
- Encouraging people to rely on church programming to take spiritual steps rather than equipping them to grow in their own faith journey.
- Adding burdens to people's lives when Jesus said we were supposed to be helping people experience joy, peace, and rest.
- Communicating that busy is better.
- Creating a works-based religion rather than offering a grace-filled relationship.
- Encouraging people to be transformed into my likeness rather than encouraging people to become more like Christ and more of who God has created them to be. (Most times, thankfully, that will look very different than who God created me to be.)

TONY MORGAN

OK, I thought I'd just admit one of the big challenges I face in ministry. Is anyone else experiencing this tension? I want more and more people to enter into a relationship with Jesus Christ, but I also want people to experience the freedom and joy and peace found in Christ. I want them to know the God who said, "I have come that they may have life, and have it to the full" (John 10:10). Are you with me?

THE LOST GENERATION?

Wired magazine interviewed Dawn Ostroff, the president of entertainment for the CW television network. Here's a brief excerpt from the interview:

> **WIRED:** Every channel drools over the 18- to 34-year-olds.
>
> **OSTORFF:** We're the only broadcast network focusing solely on this demographic. And if you think about it, all the major life events happen to people between the ages of 18 and 34. They graduate high school, go to college, get their first apartment, and buy their first car. We will have the ability to advertise to these viewers when they're going through all of this.[26]

Here are my observations and thoughts:
- There are several other major life events that typically happen during this season of life. As examples, people get married, buy their first homes, have children, and raise those children.

- Most churches focus their ministry on people that are twenty to thirty years older than this demographic.
- This demographic is leaving the church. AgapePress reported that 88 percent of children from evangelical homes are leaving the church shortly after they graduate from high school.[27]
- Sometimes I think television is more concerned with reaching this generation than churches are.
- I'm guessing it will be almost impossible for existing churches to shift their focus to target this generation. If that's true, we probably need lots of new churches to reach this generation.

If existing churches tried to focus on reaching this generation, how would our ministries have to change?

LOVE US OR HATE US

A funny thing happened at NewSpring. We presented a service on hell. In addition to a pointed message, the service included an instrumental version of the AC/DC song "Hells Bells" complete with shooting flames. This service has caused quite a stir in blogland. I guess some bloggers who are always trying to fix us came down hard on us for that one.

The reason I know this is because a local pastor caught wind of the controversy. Someone attending the church indicated that the pastor showed short clips of this service to his church and essentially used it as an opportunity to attack our ministry. I'm sure this isn't the first or last time it will happen.

The way I found out about this particular instance is because someone who used to attend that church was curious about our ministry after hearing his pastor rail against us. He found our Web site and watched the service in its entirety. What he found, of course, was a very clear, biblical message that had a huge impact on the folks who heard it. And now, that guy is attending NewSpring.

You want to know a little secret? We love controversy at NewSpring. Frankly it's our hope that lots of people love what we do. But we also hope that a few people *hate* what we do. If we don't experience these extreme reactions, we're probably not truly fulfilling God's mission for our church. Don't forget, God despises "lukewarm." We are a church for those who are unchurched or who have given up on church. If we are fully aligned with God's mission for our ministry, we are going to offend people who love the institution or their version of "the truth" more than they love the people the Truth was intended to reach. So love us or hate us, we love you.

MA BELL

Get ready for one of the dumbest branding decisions in the history of marketing. Some genius at AT&T decided to wipe out the Cingular brand. The theory was that people would prefer to have all their communications services from one provider with one name. Here's the problem—AT&T is a smelly brand. It's old. It's not trendy. I'm going to be embarrassed to carry my new, cool Blackjack phone using boring, stodgy AT&T service.

You may be familiar with Cingular. It was the top provider of wireless service in the United States. Cingular was hip. It was orange. The icon was a cool little blob character that had personality. I was eager to brag about my Cingular service because it communicated cutting edge. AT&T, on the other hand, is my parents' telephone company. You remember that company, don't you? They were the company that used to sell this service called "long distance." They used to provide their service on actual wires that would connect to phones in my parents' home—kind of like talking with a friend using two tin cans connected by a string. AT&T is so yesterday.

What am I going to do? How can I continue promoting the bleeding edge of technology if my mobile service is provided by Ma Bell? I'm going to miss the orange blob guy.

Oh, by the way, what does your brand say?

MAN CHURCH

During a visit to Phoenix, I had the opportunity to tour the campus of Christ's Church of the Valley (ccvonline.com) in Peoria, Arizona, and talk with CCV's senior pastor Don Wilson. Don launched the ministry more than twenty years ago, and now the church has an attendance of over 10,000 people each weekend.

After spending an hour with Don, two things really struck me: Don has a clear target for who he's trying to reach, and he has a laser-focused strategy. CCV is designed to reach men. Everything they do and how they do it has men in mind. Don figures if he can reach men, he can also reach their families.

TONY MORGAN

Their mission? To win, train, and send. *Win, train, and send.* We must have heard him say that a couple of dozen times. Everything they do is designed to win people to Jesus Christ, to train believers to become disciples, and to send disciples out to impact the world. *Win, train and send.* I'm guessing everyone at CCV knows the mission.

The church has an incredible campus. It's obvious they were very strategic in how it was developed. They took into consideration not only their mission but also their location. CCV has taken advantage of the Phoenix climate to create an incredibly open campus where the space outdoors is just as integral to the ministry as the space inside their facilities.

Don and the team at CCV have proven the value of having a clear mission and focused strategy. That's paying dividends in their effort to reach men (and their families) for Jesus.

MARK BATTERSON
ON KILLING COCKROACHES

BACKSTORY—Mark is the lead pastor of National Community Church with four locations in the Washington, D.C., area. In addition to holding services in Union Station only blocks from the Capitol building, National Community Church also operates Ebenezer's Coffeehouse—an innovative missions outpost for the ministry. Mark blogs at evotional.com.

TONY: Tell me about an instance when you found yourself "killing cockroaches."

MARK: I grew up in the generation that added the word "multitask" to the dictionary. One of the greatest challenges I face is "killing cockroaches," and as a church grows larger, so do the cockroaches! Last year I had eleven direct reports. That's about seven too many! So we did some structural streamlining. I need to know less and less about more and more. It's the only way I'll maintain my sanity and National Community Church will grow to its potential.

I remember an incident a few years ago when someone on our staff asked me to make a lightbulb decision. They actually wanted me to decide between sixty-watt and hundred-watt lightbulbs. That was a moment when I realized that something was terribly wrong! And it became a turning point for me. I probably tend to be a micro-manager by personality, but I've become a delegator by necessity.

TONY: What are some of the strategies you've implemented to avoid it?

MARK: One key implementation is not checking work-related e-mails on my day off. I'm not perfect at this. But I know that if I don't have healthy boundaries, I get sucked into the email vortex. I also try to close Outlook when I need to focus!

I also know that my office is the place for me to go if I want to get nothing done! So I need to schedule time out of the office to really focus, dream, and study. There are just too many cockroaches running around the office!

TONY MORGAN

TONY: What have you learned from some of these experiences?

MARK: One of the things I wrestle with is that I never want to be "too big" or "too important" to put a towel over my arm and serve. But I also have to be wise in my use of time. Years ago someone on our staff said something I'll never forget. She said, "Don't say yes just because it's hard to say no." I'm trying to say "no" more and more!

TONY: How do you help your team avoid "killing cockroaches"?

MARK: A few years ago we cut out staff meeting agendas. We were wasting our time talking about the church van and storage space. It was like having as many people as possible weigh in on insignificant issues! So we now get together to share wins, pray together, and do team building. Somehow the positive approach helps the cockroaches just go away!

MARKETING MISTAKES

I think it's funny when I hear about churches that bash marketing tactics. I've yet to find a church that doesn't use at least a few. Some churches have opted for the sign out front, a bulletin promoting ministries and upcoming events, or an ad in the local newspaper with service times. Other churches have gone even further with marketing techniques like billboards, radio spots, or viral videos. But every church I've ever connected with is, at the very least, hopeful that word-of-mouth marketing will happen when existing members invite their friends and family.

Wherever you land on this continuum and whatever you want to call it, most churches interested in fulfilling the Great Commission want more people to show up on Sunday morning—or for more folks to take the next step in their spiritual journey. So with this goal in mind, here are several marketing mistakes churches often make that you'll want to avoid as you strive to reach people:

1. *Promoting your church instead of generating a response.* No one really cares that you are First Church Such-and-Such. And no one really cares what your building looks like. Promote a message series over the church. Promote a conversation over the church. But don't promote the church or a specific ministry. Others will do that for you if it's worth promoting.

2. *Making a promise you can't keep.* The world already thinks churches are filled with hypocrites, so make sure you exceed expectations on everything you say you'll do. The easiest place to begin is with the guest experience. Are you delivering a welcoming, friendly environment? When someone takes a step to connect to your ministry, make sure your team is ready to follow through.

3. *Trying to be all things to all people.* Obviously we want the world to know Jesus, but who has God put in your world? That's who you need to reach. And more specifically, what person within your world are

TONY MORGAN

you *most likely* to reach? Design your ministry to connect with him or her. That means some people may not like your church. That's OK. God uses different ministries to reach different people.

4. *Thinking other churches are your competition.* We are competing with today's culture. That means other churches are on your team. It doesn't help if you distinguish yourself from another church. Distinguish your message from the world that people are living in. Clearly communicate why someone should connect with your church instead of spending their time doing a million other things.

5. *Publicizing church programs that compete with one another.* More choices just create more confusion. You may have lots of great programs, but the more options you provide, the less likely people will be to take a step. I know, it's counterintuitive. But you don't want a situation where your men's ministry is competing with your discipleship classes that are competing with home groups that are competing with volunteer opportunities. Figure out what you do well and what God is using today to reach people for Jesus—and do that.

The mission we are responsible for is too important for us to get lazy about the message we're communicating. So ask yourself: Are we getting a response? Can we deliver on our promises? Do we know who we're trying to reach? Is our message being heard in today's culture? Are we competing against ourselves? All of these issues matter when it comes to making sure your message is truly impacting people's lives.[28]

MARKETING WITHOUT ADVERTISING

Sometimes the best marketing plans don't involve any advertising at all. "We take those funds that might otherwise be used to shout about our service, and we put those funds instead into *improving* the service," says Jeff Bezos, CEO of Amazon.com in an article on *BusinessWeek Online*. He went on to say, "That's the philosophy we've taken from the beginning. If you do build a great experience, customers tell each other about that. Word of mouth is very powerful."[29]

MATH LESSONS

Back when my son Jacob was in third grade, part of his studies included learning arithmetic. He's a smart kid, but he doesn't enjoy doing worksheets in his schoolbooks. He does enjoy following sports, however, so we helped him start a sports card collection.

Jacob counts the cards. He studies the player stats on the backs of the cards. He looks up the value of the cards. And wouldn't you know it, in the process of enjoying his hobby, he's learning some basic mathematical principles he'll use for the rest of his life. Jacob learns math precepts much more easily if he's enjoying the learning process.

Visitors at your church are no different than Jacob. But instead of math, these people are studying for challenges they're facing in their lives. They're trying to learn basic concepts of hope, purpose, and forgiveness. The problem is, they continue to leave the church because they find it boring and irrelevant to their lives. We're forcing our visitors to complete their biblical worksheets but providing little to no enjoyment along the way.

Since when does church equal boredom? I love the book of Acts because it gives me a clear picture of what the early church was like. This group was committed to the apostles' teaching, sharing life, and prayer together. As a result, many outsiders accepted Christ and experienced a transformed life. And what's more, these people enjoyed their church experience. "They followed a daily discipline of worship in the Temple followed by meals at home, every meal a celebration, exuberant and joyful, as they praised God. People in general liked what they saw. Every day their number grew as God added those who were saved" (Acts 2:46–47 MSG).

"People in general liked what they saw" suggests that the early church was "enjoying the favor of all the people," and with that favor came growth. Based on passages like this one in Acts, I believe boredom isn't what God intended for the church. He wants us to offer an experience that's both biblical and enjoyable. To evaluate the enjoyment level of your services, consider these questions:

- Does the worship music reflect a style that the crowd appreciates?
- Is the message addressing a topic that's relevant to people's lives?

- Is there an appropriate use of humor in the service?
- Does the service flow smoothly from one element to the next?
- Are you using visual elements to capture people's attention as they engage in worship and hear the message?
- Do you periodically surprise people with something they weren't anticipating?

These are basic questions, but it's important to review them from time to time. Naysayers might argue that by offering services that people enjoy, you are ultimately just catering to our culture's consumer mind-set. The reality is that there certainly *is* a consumer mind-set in our culture, and unless we acknowledge that and deal with it, our message—the gospel message—won't be heard.

It's entirely possible to offer biblical teaching and corporate worship in a way that people actually like. If you create an enjoyable service experience, people will not only choose to return, they'll also invite their friends. When that happens, more people will hear the truth, and God may begin to add to your number daily.[30]

MEGABLOG

I'm facing inner tension in my life. Regrettably, I now have over 3,000 blog subscribers. Some might celebrate this new "megablog" status, but I'm dealing with all kinds of turmoil.

Let me explain:

TONY MORGAN

- I had a few subscribers leave my blog for smaller blogs. They were looking for a site where they could shake hands with the blogger at the end of each post.
- I've started getting complaints that I don't do enough posts for singles.
- Some folks won't subscribe to my blog because it's too "attractional." They think I need to find a way to bring my message to the people rather than expecting them to come to my site.
- I'm getting complaints that my posts should be longer and deeper. People think I'm making it too easy for folks to understand what I'm saying. Something about a camel and the eye of a needle.
- There are some people who think bloggers should only use the Times Roman font.
- Another group of people thinks it's blasphemous that I'm "targeting" church leaders with my content. They think I should be trying to reach all blog readers.
- I happen to decide on the title of each post after I've finished writing the content. I'm a post-titlest. The pre-titlests think there's a passage in Revelation someplace that suggests my post-titlest ways may make me the antichrist.
- I don't type posts with my hands raised in the air. You know what that means.

Well, I realize my blog has a lot of readers, and I'm trying to fix that. If you have suggestions on how I can make my blog smaller and healthier, I'd really appreciate it.

MOM'S WATCHING

My mom called earlier. Apparently she found my blog. It was a secret for almost an entire year, but now the cat's out of the bag. I guess my brother and sister (who also just found it recently) clued her in. Mom said she's spreading the word to all her friends back home in Piqua, Ohio. Of course, we have to remember that it doesn't take a whole lot to stir conversation in Piqua.

I'm not sure what Mom has read at this point. Little does she know that she's been mentioned several times in the past. In fact, I've written that I may smell like Mom. I'm part of the group of bloggers who has a mom. And I have an aversion to Mother's Day (see next article).

It was one thing when I found out my pastor was reading my blog. Now that I found out my *mom* is reading my blog, I have an entirely new filter to consider. It's a good reminder that whatever you say or write or do, someone will be there to observe your words and actions. That can be suffocating, or it can be very freeing to know that God has built in boundaries to protect us.

I love you Momma-Jo! Thanks for encouraging me to lead and create and embrace life passionately. Oh, and thanks for feeding me lasagna.

MOTHER'S DAY

There's one thing you should probably know about me—the fact that I have a strong aversion to traditions, particularly as they relate to holidays. Because of that, I typically hate

TONY MORGAN

going to church on holidays like Christmas and Easter and Mother's Day.

I think the reason that they bug me so much is because there are some people who *only* go to church on holidays. If churches deliver the exact same holiday message they used last year and the year before that and the year before that, these holiday-only types never hear anything new. That also means they likely never experience a message that leads them to Jesus and life transformation.

With that in mind, I recently set about trying to find a cool church somewhere in the country that wasn't advertising a traditional Mother's Day message that weekend. As you might expect, it was a pretty difficult task. There are lots of opportunities out there for those of you who are looking for a sappy "Moms are the best" service.

One of the few nontraditional services I could find was at NewSong Church in Irvine, California. Instead of doing Mother's Day, NewSong was in the middle of a series titled "Blink." Senior pastor Dave Gibbons was using this series to help people understand that the decisions they make—sometimes in the blink of an eye—can dramatically impact what happens in their lives. Sounds like that's something the annual attenders might need to hear.

I hope I haven't offended you pastors who pass out pansies to all the moms on Mother's Day weekend. Your ministry will probably survive the experience but, really, you should have called 1-800-ASK-TONY.

Word to your mother.

MTV: SHOULD WE JUST IGNORE IT?

I watched the MTV Music Video Awards and posted my reaction on my blog. That generated some great questions and comments. Some are asking why it should matter what happens on MTV? Specifically, Brenton asked, "What percentage of society does MTV really represent?" I think it's a valid question. With that in mind, here are some specific answers from the Cabletelevision Advertising Bureau (CAB):

- MTV is the #1 media brand in the world.
- It is the favorite and most watched network for teens ages 12 to 19.
- MTV targets young adults ages 18 to 34 who represent 29 percent of the U.S. population.[31]

A previous profile from CAB said this about MTV: "MTV's median age is exactly when a majority of young American adults begin to form lifelong brand loyalties. Young adults 15–17 are excited consumers and extremely impressionable. Now is the time to influence their choices."[32] This information about MTV is alarming if you also consider these facts:

- 88 percent of children from evangelical homes are leaving the church shortly after they graduate from high school.[33]
- 49 percent of Boomers, 43 percent of Busters and 33 percent of Mosaics attend church on a given Sunday.[34] Notice a trend?

- "Denominations and youth workers have estimated that between 65 percent and 94 percent of their high school students stop attending church after they graduate."[35]
- Dr. Frank Page, former Southern Baptist Convention president, said, "It's a disturbing trend, and part of it is that our churches have become one- or two-generation churches, and we've failed to learn how to reach out to this younger generation."[36]

We can continue ignoring MTV and their audience. We can complain about their programming that influences young lives. We can explain all the reasons why their music doesn't fit in our services. We can argue why their issues and questions are not appropriate for our messages. That same MTV audience, however, seems to be ignoring the church.

MUSIC

Music has always been an important part of my life. Both my parents were music majors in college. My dad was a high school band director. I play piano and used to play several other instruments. I've enjoyed following music since I was a child. Music was there during the celebrations and the sorrow. There are songs that come on the radio that take me back to the days when Emily and I first started dating and dancing. Music is powerful in my life, and I happen to believe it plays an important part of many other people's lives both inside and outside of the church.

With that, I found an article about the band The Fray in

an issue of *Relevant* magazine to be pretty intriguing. Here's what Ben Wysocki, the band's drummer, had to say about Christian music:

"As Christians, we set out to make really honest art that is relatable and understandable for people, regardless of their religious orientation or faith background. Isaac grew up writing Christian songs in a Christian language about Christian themes and Bible verses, and then he started making friends who weren't Christians, and they couldn't understand what he was singing about. They couldn't relate to it. We wanted to steer clear of those labels and a lot of baggage and make art in a way that can relate to Christians and non-Christians."

He continued, "I think we're called to make music for more than just the Church and to make music for the unchurched people and hopefully speak a bit of life into them."[37]

We tend to think the music we play in church has to tie up all the loose ends and have all the answers. I've found, however, that some of the most powerful messages were preached following songs that were written by "secular" artists that raised lots of questions about life. You'd be amazed at how often Top 40 music touches on issues that are, at their core, of a spiritual nature. They may not be singing about the name of Jesus, but they're talking about topics that the Bible addresses. And frankly, I think sometimes those songs are much better for preparing a congregation to hear biblical truth about real-life issues than the most well-known hymns and worship songs.

What do you think? Should Christ followers use music to "speak a bit of life" into those who are unchurched? And is

TONY MORGAN

it acceptable to use that type of music in church services? In case you're wondering, I do.

NELSON SEARCY
ON KILLING COCKROACHES

BACKSTORY—Nelson is the lead pastor of a multicultural church called The Journey Church with locations in Manhattan, Brooklyn, and Jersey City. Part of The Journey's unique story is that they have 1,200 people gathering in small groups. That's amazing for a church that has a weekly attendance of about 1,100 people. You can stay connected with Nelson's coaching network by visiting churchleaderinsights.com.

If you are constantly killing cockroaches, it's because you've created a system where this is allowed. If you are able to consistently focus on your highest and most important tasks, then it's because you've created a system where *this* is allowed. So how do you help people around you know when you're available and when you're focused on your highest and most important tasks? I'm certainly more of a student than a model for this, but here's what I've learned along the way:

- *Never promise "all access."* You don't have to say you are "not available." Just don't consistently say you *are* available. If someone wants to talk with you after a church service, talk with them right then and there. Don't say to "call my office to schedule an appointment" unless that's what you really want to do. An on-the-spot investment of time and prayer may save you hours in the long run.

- *Train your assistant to handle all requests for meetings,* and let him or her serve as a gate-keeper. It takes the right personality on their part and clear communication on your part, but it's a beautiful thing when it happens.

- *Meet regularly with your key people,* and make sure they are prepared for the meetings. Teach your key people to keep a list of what needs to be discussed when you meet. You should do the same so you don't become *their* cockroach. Meetings are the best time-saving devise ever invented. Meetings are the playground of highly effective ministry teams. The problem is not with "meetings" but with how meetings are run. You must learn how to hold an effective meeting and train your people to do the same.

- *Teach your people the best way for them to communicate with you.* I train my staff to ask these questions:

1. Is this something that needs Nelson's involvement right now? For example, is there someone else to talk to first?

TONY MORGAN

2. Is this something that can wait until our next scheduled meeting? If so, write it down.
3. Is this something I can e-mail and get a response from him later?
4. Is this a phone call? Sometimes a phone call, instead of a personal meeting, is the best way to save time and manage communication.
5. Is this something that has to be done with Nelson right now? If so, let's deal with it.

I have been a student of time management since I was sixteen years old, and I am passionate about it. I hire people who fit my time management approach. What we do is too important to be killing cockroaches.

NOISE

Seth Godin caught my attention with a blog post referencing a *Washington Post* article.[38] The article describes a unique performance arranged by the newspaper. They asked Joshua Bell, a Grammy award-winning violinist, to play his violin at a Washington, D.C., metro stop for nearly forty-five minutes. More than a thousand people passed by during that time, but almost no one stopped to hear him play.

Though Seth made the comparison with marketing, the similarities are even more striking to me with our efforts to share the gospel message. Rather than masterpieces by Bach and Schubert that "have endured for centuries," we share what many, including myself, believe to be the greatest story ever told. And like many great performers, we assume that ordinary people will recognize the power of our message since it's inspired by God himself. Here are a handful of parallels that jumped out at me as I was reading the article:

- If a great classical musician can use one of the finest instruments ever crafted and play some of the greatest music ever written and not be heard, there's a chance even the best communicators in ideal venues sharing the greatest message also will not be heard.
- For some people, it doesn't matter if it's "one of the most difficult violin pieces to master." If the message doesn't relate to their world, they probably won't hear it, no matter how "deep" it is.
- The violinist didn't connect with his crowd. "He seems so apart from his audience—unseen, unheard, otherworldly—that you find yourself thinking that he's not really there." Similarly, it's possible to preach a biblical message and not be heard.
- "Context matters." With a symphony, the violinist would likely receive an ovation. At a metro stop, however, the same violinist is ignored. Our message must also have context. That's why we use stories and the arts to connect with people and make our message relevant to their lives.
- Bell explained, "I'm surprised at the number of people who don't pay attention at all, as if I'm invisible. Because you know what? I'm makin' a lot of noise!" How many times have we tried to explain something a little more

TONY MORGAN

clearly or yell just a little bit louder hoping someone would hear us?

- The primary reason people didn't stop to hear the violinist was because "they were busy" and "had other things on their mind." Those are the exact same barriers that prevent people from hearing our message. We can either try to yell louder (and most likely be ignored), or we can try to more effectively connect with busy people who are consumed with the grinding details of their lives.

- They didn't stop to hear the violinist—"not because people didn't have the capacity to understand beauty, but because it was irrelevant to them." Sometimes I think we need to be less concerned about whether or not we're teaching the right message and more concerned with whether or not we're addressing people's needs. Jesus modeled that for us.

One of my favorite passages in Scripture is Romans 10. It's always been a great reminder to me of my calling as a Christ follower and as a minister. "How can they believe in the one of whom they have not heard? And how can they hear without someone preaching to them?" (Rom. 10:14). Stories like this, though, challenge me to look at this passage in a whole new light. Is it possible to preach the gospel message and not be heard? If people don't come to faith, is it just noise? If lives aren't transformed, does the message even matter?

"Joshua Bell was standing there playing at rush hour, and people were not stopping, and not even looking, and some were flipping quarters at him!" I'm just not satisfied with that response. I want people to experience God's forgiveness and love the way I experience it. That's why I work so diligently not only to make sure we're preaching God's Word but that we're offering it in a way that connects with the people we're trying to reach.

NOTHING, ARIZONA

So I'm reading Robert Scoble's blog (scobleizer.com), and I come across his post about Google's lack of strategy actually *being* a strategy.[39] It reminded me of my visit to Nothing, Arizona. You probably haven't heard of Nothing, Arizona, because it's essentially . . . nothing. Here's the sign that hangs in the center of the town:

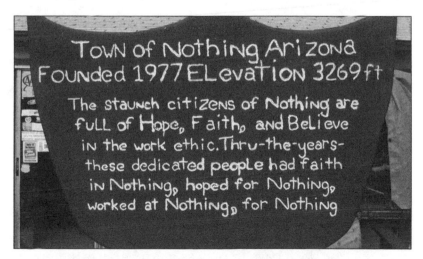

Town of Nothing Arizona
Founded 1977 Elevation 3269 ft
The staunch citizens of Nothing are full of Hope, Faith, and Believe in the work ethic. Thru-the-years- these dedicated people had faith in Nothing, hoped for Nothing, worked at Nothing, for Nothing

As you can see, the people of Nothing had a vision for Nothing that involved nothing. There's really not much to the town of Nothing. There's a gas station called the "All

TONY MORGAN

Mart" and a couple of trailers. Nothing was their vision, and it resulted in nothing. Well, these thoughts about lack of vision, or a vision of nothing, got me in a particularly feisty mood, and I began to list some of the advantages of doing ministry without a ministry strategy. Here are:

✦ ✦ 10 ADVANTAGES OF DOING MINISTRY ✦ ✦ WITHOUT A MINISTRY STRATEGY

1. You give the loudest person the opportunity to decide what happens at your church.
2. Sharp leaders who are accustomed to serving in organizations with clearly defined plans for future growth won't stick around your church. That means more ministry for you!
3. You'll get to hone your debating skills as people argue about what to do next.
4. More meetings! Where there's no strategy, the meetings flourish.
5. Some call them church splits. We like to call them church plants. More mother churches!
6. You don't have to worry about celebrating success because no one even knows what success looks like. It's just better to keep that a secret.
7. Rather than trying to discern God's will for your ministry, you can just rely on dumb luck.
8. You don't have to pray as much because there's nothing to pray for. As an added bonus, that means you don't have to develop as much faith either. Whatever happens . . . happens.

9. You can count your offerings faster because people will save their financial gifts for organizations that actually have a plan for the money they receive.
10. Your lack of ministry strategy, which *is* a ministry strategy, will do just fine in Nothing, Arizona.

I probably shouldn't write when I'm in a feisty mood, should I? Regardless of how you answer that question, I still recommend that you don't vacation in Nothing, Arizona and don't do ministry without a ministry strategy.

Thank you, Robert Scoble. And thanks for Nothing.

ONE LIFE

Jud Wilhite, the senior pastor of Central Christian Church (centralchristian.com) in Las Vegas, recently stopped in at NewSpring. For those unfamiliar with Jud's story, he took over at Central when Gene Appel left to join the leadership team at Willow Creek Community Church (willowcreek.org) in South Barrington, Illinois. Jud inherited a forty-year-old ministry and followed an incredible transition that occurred under Appel's leadership. In the last few years, though, Central has continued to grow under Jud's leadership. They've jumped from around 7,000 people to more than 12,000 people in attendance each weekend.

Jud hung out with our leadership team while we met for our weekly senior management team meeting. It was encouraging to hear the stories from Central, including

TONY MORGAN

the success of their first multisite campus in Summerlin, Nevada. Within a year of that campus launching, they already had 2,000 people attending each weekend. In fact, 60 to 70 percent of the folks who attend the Summerlin campus have never attended a service at their original Henderson campus. Central is obviously reaching a completely new audience with their second campus.

During the time we spent with Jud, he also shared these leadership nuggets. He encouraged us to:

- *Plan for the "one life."* He said we need to always keep in mind the one friend or family member we are praying for to receive Christ into their life. Consider this "one life" as you're preparing a weekend service or any other ministry outreach to confirm that your teaching and experience speak to that person.
- *Structure around "growth engines."* Central's growth engines are the weekend services, family ministry, campus ministries, groups, and leadership development. Their entire ministry is structured around those key areas, and they have one identified leader over each of those areas.
- *Focus your ministry.* Jud indicated that for their church, this means simplifying their ministry programming to focus on weekends, groups, and serving. That's it. They have tried to eliminate anything else that might compete with these primary ways that people take their next steps toward Christ.

I'm grateful for the time and encouragement he gave our team. It confirmed again that I still have a lot to learn from other leaders.

PANIC AT THE HOTEL

Prior to moving to South Carolina, I made a trip with Mark, one of my former ministry teammates at Granger Community Church. Among other things, Mark is a pastor, a fellow author, and a merciful traveling partner. Unbeknownst to him, Mark became a key supporting actor in one of the most embarrassing episodes of my life.

It all began after I finished my workout at the gym. Since I didn't want to stink for the dinner we had scheduled later that evening, I decided to grab a quick shower. I had just finished lathering my back with the more than adequate bar of hotel soap when I turned to rinse off. In the process of trying to turn around in the shower, I lost my footing.

At that moment my thoughts began to slow precipitously. First, I realized I was slipping. Then I realized, "Hey, I'm not going to be able to regain my footing." Then I realized, "Hey, I'm going to fall in the bathtub." Then I began to realize, "No, there's no way I'm going to land in the bathtub." I grabbed for the shower curtain. I'm not sure why I did that. There was a large bar on the shower wall. Someone probably wisely put it there for people like me who have a propensity to fall when making sharp pivots in the bathtub. But regrettably, my instinct wasn't to grab the bar.

TONY MORGAN

Instead I grasped what I could of the shower curtain. That was helpful for a moment. It slowed the fall, but then the curtain ripped off the shower rod. By this time my body was flailing wildly across the bathroom. By the time I came to rest, I was lodged somewhere between the bathtub and the toilet. The shower curtain was on the other side of the bathroom under the sink. The shower was still on. And my back was still well-lathered.

Honestly the first thought that ran through my mind at this point wasn't, "Am I OK? Am I hurt?" And I wasn't thinking, "Man, I'm fortunate. I could have hit my head and be in bad shape right now." My first thought was this: "Dear God, I will never make fun of people who listen to country music again. Just don't let Mark come in here to make sure I'm OK and see me sprawled out naked on the bathroom floor."

At that point I lifted myself from the bathroom floor and tried to at least turn off the water so that it wasn't spraying all over the place. Instead of turning the water off, though, I inadvertently turned the water temperature to its hottest setting. Of course, I didn't realize this until I had the curtain in my hand and was trying to reattach it to the shower rod. I scorched my right foot. But I should point out, my back was still well-lathered.

By the time I was fully recovered and fully rinsed, I ended up with minor scrapes on my back and a very red right foot. The only thing that was truly damaged was my ego. But honestly I'm a little concerned about my relationship with Mark. I wondered several times afterward, "What if I was really hurt? How long would Mark have waited before he came and found

KILLING COCKROACHES

out if I was really OK?" I guess I've found that you learn who your true friends are when you are sprawled out naked on the bathroom floor of a hotel room. To Mark's credit, he did provide this very detailed sketch to graphically represent my verbal description of "the fall."

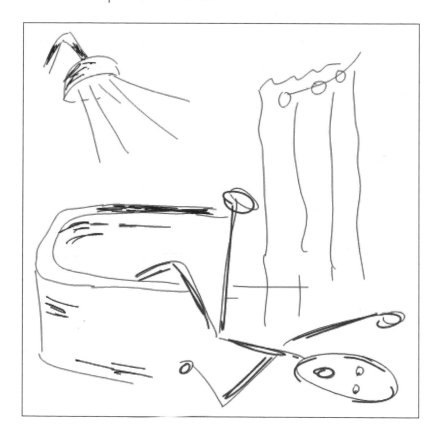

By the way, I've executed all the pivots in the bathtub flawlessly since this episode, without incident. My new streak of showers taken without falling is still intact.

At this point I could try to redeem this embarrassing moment of my life to help make a compelling spiritual or leadership principle come to life. I could challenge you to

TONY MORGAN

consider the places in your life where you need to be naked or vulnerable. I could encourage you to consider the people in your life who may be falling that you don't know about. I could use this as an opportunity to talk about embracing the artistic gifting of people like Mark.

Honestly, though, I know that any attempt on my part to turn the corner and provide life application will certainly be overshadowed by the haunting image of this episode that is now permanently etched in your mind.

PARACHUTE PANTS

So I'm having lunch with a few folks including this guy I just met who happens to be in his senior year of college. We were chatting about several topics including baseball, ministry, and job hunting. He mentioned that his dad was a pastor. Before I could catch myself I asked the question, "Is he still pastoring?"

Here's what's funny about that question. Until that point in the conversation, I was viewing this guy as my peer. I asked the question because I just assumed this guy's dad must be getting close to retirement. I was wondering whether or not he was still in the ministry or if, like my dad, he was retired and spending a lot of time on the golf course.

As soon as the question had slipped through my lips, the reality finally hit me—this sharp guy who is soon to be graduating and getting married and has the whole world in front of him is young enough to be my child. He's just a punk kid. His "close to retirement" dad is my age.

I don't know what happened, but sometime between putting on my last pair of parachute pants and today's lunch, I became the old guy.

It was just another harsh reminder that life here on earth is brief. If we're going to make our lives count, we'd better figure out how to begin today. We also need to continue to raise up sharp "punk kids" and equip them to lead. Instead of telling them where to go, we'd better listen and learn and empower them to reach the next generation.

For what it's worth, it's good that I already know how to play golf. It makes the transition to old guy a lot easier. I'm just praying The Buckle comes out with a line of hip golf attire before too long.

PENELOPE TRUNK ON KILLING COCKROACHES

BACKSTORY—Penelope Trunk is a career columnist at the *Boston Globe*. Her syndicated column has run in more than two hundred publications. Earlier she was a software executive, then she founded two companies. She has been through an IPO, an acquisition, and a bankruptcy. Before that she played professional beach volleyball. Her book is *Brazen Careerist: The New Rules for Success*.

TONY: Tell me about an instance when you found yourself "killing cockroaches."

PENELOPE: I kill cockroaches every day because

it's easier than doing the hard stuff on my to-do list. Especially if I'm wearing shoes with a thick sole. Just scrunch, right? I get up in the morning, and my to-do list is organized with the most important stuff written on top and the other nonthreatening stuff on the bottom, and I so frequently spend my time on the bottom, on the stuff that is small and squishable with just one stomp.

TONY: What are some of the strategies you've implemented to avoid it?

PENELOPE: I try to check in with myself emotionally. If I'm not doing the hard stuff, I ask myself why. Sometimes I'm feeling anxious or I'm premenstrual or I just yelled at my kids and I think I've ruined their lives (for the millionth time) and I need to just let myself wander up and down my to-do list doing easy stuff. I need a break. But sometimes I look at what I'm doing and I say, "I have more strength right now. Don't squander it." And I go to the top of the list and do the hardest thing. Sometimes I need a warm up. Like right now. Answering these questions is not the toughest thing I have to do today, but it's harder than, say, answering the e-mails where people tell me they loved my last post and I'm great. So I picked this task because I knew I'd feel accomplished at the end because it is challenging but it's not so challenging that I couldn't face it. It is my bridge to the hard stuff today.

TONY: What have you learned from some of these experiences?

PENELOPE: If I spend too much time on the stuff that doesn't matter, I feel like I did nothing. Killing one cockroach is OK because maybe you are helping someone else (after all, the woman in your office that day was screaming) and sometimes you are helping yourself (we each have times when we are silently screaming). But killing cockroaches all day feels dirty. (Yes, I know, cockroaches are the cleanest insects around.) We feel dirty because it is actually squandering our passion and energy to spend a day doing nothing to promote our vision for what our work is about. The big-picture, tough stuff that we keep an eye on is what makes us feel good about our work, I think.

TONY: How do you help your team avoid "killing cockroaches"?

PENELOPE: I hire great people so that they think as hard about this stuff as I do. It's nearly impossible to really know what we are supposed to be doing with our days to make life matter. But I love being around people who are asking themselves this question every day. A team of people like this means that everyone is trying to do some of the hard stuff every day—without me telling them to. So then my job is to show people how I'm trying to do it every day. I get inspired by this set of questions right here. We can inspire each other with an honest struggle to have meaningful days. But only if we surround ourselves with people who are engaged in asking good questions. So thanks for this, Tony.

TONY MORGAN

PHIL COOKE
ON KILLING COCKROACHES

BACKSTORY—Called a "media guru" by *Christianity Today* magazine, Phil is CEO and creative director of Cooke Pictures and founding partner of TWC Films— a company that produced two commercials for the 2008 Super Bowl. He's also the author of the book *Branding Faith: Why Some Churches and Non-Profits Impact Culture and Others Don't.*

In working with media leaders, one of my most important "commandments" is to spend less time on what's urgent and more time on what matters. In my case, I've mastered e-mail. In fact, you could say I'm a Jedi-Knight of e-mail. I can do it over a wireless network, cell network, or from any computer on the planet.

But a few years ago I was filming in London, and while my wife and I waited in the hotel for the crew to bring the vehicles around, I went to the lobby restroom. While standing at the urinal, I noticed a British businessman standing at the urinal next to me, except in his *other* hand he was holding his BlackBerry and checking e-mails.

I leaned over to him and said, "Buddy, that's bondage." He leaned back and in a perfect British accent said, "Sir, you have no idea."

I walked out of that restroom and handed my wife my Blackberry and haven't touched it since. I decided

I never want to become so addicted to e-mails that I need to check it while going to the restroom.

Technology is a wonderful tool, but ultimately it's not about the tool. It's about what we accomplish *with* the tool. At the judgment seat, Jesus won't say, "Hey, Phil, you did a great job with those e-mails." He'll ask if I accomplished my purpose and calling.

What leash (or cockroach) is holding you back from your destiny?

PRACTICE MAKES BETTER

I read a fascinating quote from K. Anders Ericsson, professor of psychology at Florida State University, in *Fast Company* magazine. He was talking about the importance of practice.

"Successful people spontaneously do things differently from those individuals who stagnate. They have different practice histories. Elite performers engage in what we call 'deliberate practice'—an effortful activity designed to improve individual target performance. There has to be some way they're innovating in the way they do things."[40]

As I read that, it made me think about ways I'm trying to be disciplined in my life to become successful. In case you're curious, here are some ways I'm currently "deliberately practicing" to improve my performance:

- I'm reading through the Bible again and posting my notes on my blog to keep me focused (and hopefully encourage you).

TONY MORGAN

- I've scheduled a two-week vacation with my family to relax and renew and build new memories together.
- I'm reading through *The E-Myth Revisited* with my ministry team at the encouragement of a couple of guys from North Point Community Church (northpoint.org).
- I'm exercising regularly. Recently ran three and a half miles at a nine-minute pace. That's good for me.

I don't know about you, but I tend to get sloppy when I'm not disciplined. When that happens, I don't perform at full strength. It also impacts how I relate with others. But the good thing is that God wants to help us remain disciplined. This comes through in the encouragement Timothy gave to those with the gift of teaching: "Be diligent in these matters; give yourself wholly to them, so that everyone may see your progress. Watch your life and doctrine closely. Persevere in them, because if you do, you will save both yourself and your hearers" (I Tim. 4:15–16).

What a great reminder! The disciplines in my life not only impact who I am, but they also impact others around me.

PROGRAMS DON'T WORK

Joe Schimmels, the lead pastor of Blue Sky Church (blueskychurch.com) in Loveland, Colorado, was recently listening to George Barna speak. He relayed this:

"As I sat hearing him speak, he said, 'Our research shows that transformation does not occur in the church.' In context, he was referring to all of our events, programs, and activities."[41]

What a challenge! In our desire to help people become fully devoted followers of Christ, we think we need to get them to experience a ministry program, retreat, or class at the church. And yet research is showing that these activities don't lead to transformation. Barna is focusing his attention more on home church and group experiences. Again, in my mind this suggests that relational connection must be the key ingredient. The problem is that encouraging people to step into those types of relationships is much harder than just inviting people to show up for an event at the church.

Is anyone else frustrated by realities like this? I desperately want people to experience life transformation. I want people to pursue Jesus and be radically committed to him. Yet when we try to create experiences at the church to help people along that path, the research shows it's not going to help. Argh! Frustrating!

Why can't people experience spiritual transformation through methods that work best for me? Life would be so much easier.

PROVOCATIVE?

Our church isn't competing with other churches for people's attention. Instead we're competing with everything that people choose to focus on at any given moment. And honestly, the normal person is rarely thinking about our ministry or our message. Our message may be important, but it won't capture people's attention if it's not compelling. Kathy Sierra described it this way:

TONY MORGAN

"So this isn't about having to bribe people into paying attention by sexing things up with graphics, sound, or shock. This is about helping the mind and the brain agree on what's worth paying attention to. And if you want it to be you, then you better be the most provocative and interesting thing in their environment."[42]

Who are you trying to reach with your message? Are they paying attention? If not, the easy thing to do is blame them for not listening. The harder thing to do is to determine how you might compel them to fully engage in your message.

QUESTIONS

Mavericks at Work, a book by Bill Taylor and Polly LaBarre, inspired a few questions that I think apply to churches. Here are their questions retooled for ministries. We should probably be asking ourselves:

1. Does my church provide such a unique experience and ministry to our community that it can't be provided nearly as well by any other organization?

2. Has my church created a place to serve that's so dynamic, most employees or volunteers would be hard-pressed to find a similar environment somewhere else?

3. Has my church forged a uniquely emotional (dare I say spiritual) connection with guests that other organizations can't replicate?

4. All of those questions lead to this final one: If your church closed its doors tomorrow, would anyone really miss you and why?

I want to challenge you to wrestle with these questions as a leadership team. Take some time to pause the daily grind and consider the real impact your ministry is having on people's lives and your community as a whole.

READY FOR CHANGE?

I know you too well. You crave the Top 10 lists. They make your brain happy. With that in mind, here's a list that's been percolating in my head. It applies in ministry, but I know it also applied when I was leading in the marketplace. Here are:

✦ ✦ 10 SIGNS YOU'RE NOT READY FOR CHANGE ✦ ✦

1. You see other organizations as competition instead of idea incubators.
2. You're trying to avoid criticism that comes when you fail . . . and when you succeed.
3. You're afraid of the culture.
4. Your life is fast and cluttered, and there's no space to dream.
5. You value getting it right over getting started.
6. You believe conflict is a bad thing.
7. You've stopped asking questions.
8. You think systems and strategy are the enemies of creativity.

TONY MORGAN

9. You're expecting to receive credit for your ideas.

10. You think you've already arrived.

The question is less about whether or not your organization is ready for change. The bigger question is—are *you* ready for change?

REAL NEEDS OF REAL PEOPLE

One of my favorite chapters in the Bible is Romans 10. I love it because Paul clearly reveals how we can enter into a relationship with Jesus Christ (verse 9), but he also tells us how we can have an impact on the lives of others through the teaching of God's Word. "Faith comes from hearing the message, and the message is heard through the word of Christ" (verse 17). That's powerful and challenging for me. It's part of what drives me to encourage other churches to become more effective in helping people meet Jesus and experience life transformation.

If we can help more people hear the message, then more people will come to faith in Jesus. So how can we help them hear the message? That's where it gets more challenging, particularly in today's culture with so many well-packaged, competing messages that are pulling people away from God. It's becoming harder and harder for people just to hear our message—the message of forgiveness, hope, and love found only in Jesus Christ. How do we get more people to listen?

Well, it shouldn't surprise you to know that I believe Jesus has revealed some insights to help us with this mission. You're probably aware that Jesus did some teaching. Of course, one of his most famous messages was the Sermon on the Mount. We'll look at that in a moment, but I think the verses that precede that message give us a clue as to how we can get more people to hear the message. As Matthew 4:23 says, "Jesus went throughout Galilee, teaching in their synagogues, preaching the good news of the kingdom, and healing every disease and sickness among the people." I think it's interesting that Jesus was not only teaching, he was addressing the real needs of real people. In fact, I don't think it's a stretch to say people listened to Jesus teach because he first listened to the people's needs.

And that carried over into the message he taught on the mountainside. While he was teaching, he really wasn't continuing his physical healings, but through his teaching he was offering emotional and relational healing. He understood people's needs, and he addressed them through his teaching. Anger. Sex. Money. Worry. He was teaching about the real issues of real lives.

When our goal is spiritual growth instead of outreach, the approach we take to sharing the message can change. We can begin with God's Word rather than felt needs, helping people learn to apply the truth to their lives. But when our primary goal is to help people meet Jesus for the very first time, we need to remember that those people are not looking for a three-point message that exegetes the biblical text. More knowledge won't help. They're trying to parent their kids, save their marriages, deal with losses and illnesses and addictions. They're trying to find purpose and fulfillment for their lives.

TONY MORGAN

Because of that, we need to ask ourselves, "Is our message relevant to their lives?" When that happens, our message has the potential not only to be heard but also to transform.

RED-LETTER WORDS

In some translations of the Bible, Jesus' words are printed using red ink. So as I've been studying lately, focusing on just the red words, I've been considering what Jesus has really asked me to do. I've started listing out the action words Jesus spoke. Here are some examples of the red-letter words that are shaping who I have become and where I'm going:

- *Believe*—"I assure you, anyone who believes in me already has eternal life" (John 6:47 NLT).
- *Turn*—"Turn from your sins and turn to God, because the Kingdom of Heaven is near" (Matt. 4:17 NLT).
- *Follow*—"If any of you wants to be my follower, you must put aside your selfish ambition, shoulder your cross daily, and follow me" (Luke 9:23 NLT).
- *Thirst*—"Blessed are those who hunger and thirst for righteousness" (Matt. 5:6).
- *Give*—"Give to everyone who asks you, and if anyone takes what belongs to you, do not demand it back" (Luke 6:30).
- *Forgive*—"If you forgive those who sin against you, your heavenly Father will forgive you. But if you refuse to forgive others, your Father will not forgive your sins" (Matt. 6:14–15 NLT).

- *Ask*—"Ask, using my name, and you will receive, and you will have abundant joy" (John 16:24 NLT).
- *Agree*—"I also tell you this: If two of you agree down here on earth concerning anything you ask, my Father in heaven will do it for you" (Matt. 18:19 NLT).
- *Serve*—"Whoever wants to be a leader among you must be your servant, and whoever wants to be first must be the slave of all. For even I, the Son of Man, came here not to be served but to serve others, and to give my life as a ransom for many" (Mark 10:43–45 NLT).
- *Love*—"'You must love the Lord your God with all your heart, all your soul, all your mind, and all your strength.' The second is equally important: 'Love your neighbor as yourself.' No other commandment is greater than these" (Mark 12:30–31 NLT).
- *Pray*—"This is how you should pray: 'Father, may your name be honored. May your Kingdom come soon. Give us our food day by day. And forgive us our sins—just as we forgive those who have sinned against us. And don't let us yield to temptation'" (Luke 11:2–4 NLT).
- *Worship*—"The time is coming and is already here when true worshipers will worship the Father in spirit and in truth. The Father is looking for anyone who will worship him that way" (John 4:23 NLT).
- *Obey*—"Blessed rather are those who hear the word of God and obey it" (Luke 11:28).
- *Seek*—"Seek his kingdom, and these things will be given to you as well" (Luke 12:31).

- *Trust*—"Do not let your hearts be troubled. Trust in God" (John 14:1).
- *Go*—"Go and make disciples of all the nations, baptizing them in the name of the Father and the Son and the Holy Spirit. Teach these new disciples to obey all the commands I have given you. And be sure of this: I am with you always, even to the end of the age" (Matt. 28:19–20 NLT).

Pretty simple. I'm trying to better understand these sixteen red-letter words and apply them to my life. That's God's will. He wants that for me. That's where I find his purpose for my life. That's where I experience joy.

RESPONSIVENESS

Responsiveness is not just about *individual* success. It's also a key ingredient to your success as a ministry organization. If your church (meaning your staff and volunteers) doesn't respond to phone calls, e-mail messages, Web inquiries, and information kiosk requests, people assume that you don't care or they think your church is too big. Responsiveness matters, and it *really* matters in the church.

Michael Hyatt, president and CEO of Thomas Nelson Publishers, said it this way: "The truth is, you are building your reputation—your brand—one response at a time. People are shaping their view of you by how you respond to them."[43]

Put yourself in the shoes of every person who's trying to connect to your ministry. Analyze every touchpoint. Do you get a follow up call? Are e-mail messages responded to within twenty-four hours? If you volunteer, then does someone make sure you get connected? Is your investment of time valued? All of these questions matter in ministry because people will always be consumers before they become committed.

RIPPING OTHER CHURCHES

You may have wondered: Why is it that Tony only says good things about other churches? I know. My blog rankings would probably go up if I used my site to rip apart other ministries like some other bloggers do. Arguments increase blog traffic. Obviously I don't agree with or support everything every church does, but there are a lot of great churches doing some incredible ministry throughout the country. I like to point that out from time to time. That's a lot more fun for me than trying to provide all the doctrinal and theological reasons why people should avoid going to a particular church.

This brings to mind an e-mail message I received from a woman who told of waking up depressed in a new town, far from home, disconnected from family and friends and the normal drumbeat of her life. Feeling very lonely, she prayed that God would help her somehow become engaged in this new place and culture. It had been a long time since she'd been in church. But her newfound distance from all things familiar made her wish for a church to attend—just to get out of the house if nothing else.

Browsing the Internet, she happened to stumble across my Web site, which happened to include a mention about a church near her. (Funny how these things just "happen.") It became her point of contact with God's people worshiping just down the road, people who could enter her life and welcome her into theirs, people who could meet her at a place of real fear and vulnerability, and minister to her at the deepest levels of need.

So my blog rankings may be lower because I choose to build up rather than beat down other churches, but at least it was helpful in connecting one lonely woman with a great church. I hope she's not the last.

RISKS

This evening after dinner, Brooke, our youngest daughter, wanted to jump up on our oldest daughter's lap. As you might guess, any leap for a two-year-old involves a lot of risk. So before the big jump, she blurted out, "Don't fall me down."

I guess fear of taking risks is something we learn at an early age. But when so much joy and accomplishment can be experienced through the risks we take in life, why is it that we learn to fear them? It all comes down to trust. If you know that someone you love and trust is going to catch you, you apparently are willing to take bigger risks. Knowing this, of course, causes control freaks like me to question how much faith we really have in a sovereign God. Is it wrong for me to admit that sometimes I'm afraid to leap because I'm worried God won't be there to catch me?

There is a leadership lesson here as well. People are looking for security before they're willing to risk. They want to know that if they fail, someone will be there to pick them up. Does it make you wonder who on your team is ready to leap? It should. What would you be willing to do if you knew someone would be there to "don't fall you down"?

ROCK STAR

I get to hang out with cool people every day. There's no question about it—I serve on a team of rock stars. They love Jesus. They love the ministry. They're high capacity. They're passionate about what they do. They always give their best. They stretch me to be a better leader. I love my team. But not everyone can be a rock star. Some of us get to practice the fine art of humility more than others. So here are:

✦ ✦ 10 SIGNS THAT YOU ARE NOT A ROCK STAR ✦ ✦

1. There is no opening act.
2. Your wife and your kids are your only groupies.
3. You tried out for your bowling team in college and made the team.
4. You used to play baritone in the marching band.
5. Your "crib" is located in Anderson, South Carolina.
6. You used to cruise chicks in a Dodge Omni.
7. You golf.
8. You get interviewed by *Church Executive* magazine instead of *Rolling Stone*.
9. The crowd hasn't asked for an encore.
10. You used to be in a band called Burning Heart.

TONY MORGAN

Yes, that's me. I'm the second guy in from the left. Don't you just love the look? Jacket with jeans. That may work. But what's up with the bow tie? And for goodness sake, it's a good thing someone invented hair product. These were the pre-gel days. In case you're not familiar with Burning Heart, we were the rage in church basements throughout southwest Ohio in the late 1980s.

God has uniquely wired me for certain roles in ministry. I can assure you, being a musician in a band wasn't one of them. This is a good reminder that one of my most important roles as a leader is to help my teammates (and me) match who they are with the roles they play. When that happens, it benefits the ministry. Staff and volunteers have a better chance of finding fulfillment as they serve. And it's more likely that you'll *also* be surrounded by a team of rock stars.

KILLING COCKROACHES

RULES GET IN THE WAY

I grew up in a religious tradition that was focused on following the rules rather than entering into a relationship with Jesus. Maybe it's because of this baggage I had growing up that I'm very cognizant of the pitfalls and stumbling blocks that "rule-following" can create for people who are looking at the church from the outside and thinking either "I'm not good enough to join them" or "If it's just about following rules, I don't *want* to join them."

Once you get inside the church, I've learned that "rule-creating" and "rule-following" tend to foster division and suck the life out of worship and relationships. Obedience to God's Word is one thing. It's certainly a good thing to pursue Jesus and holiness. But creating and forcing people to follow man-made rules is damaging to the faith and to the church.

The irony of "rule-creating" and "rule-following" is that it is often a reflection of the pride in our lives that makes us think we always know what's right and that others don't. (Isn't it ironic that you won't find many people creating rules about pride?)

The reality, of course, is that we have great freedom in Christ. If you don't believe me, just spend some time studying the book of Galatians. That book is a loud warning to us to be careful about mixing legalism into our faith. In fact, you may also want to study how many times Jesus *rebuked* the "rule-creators" and the "rule-followers." You'll be amazed at how often Jesus challenged the religious leaders while at the same time showing compassion to those who admitted they were broken and hurting and lost.

TONY MORGAN

Because of this, I'm grateful for ministries like Mecklenburg Community Church (mecklenburg.org). This church is pastored by James Emery White, and they are located in Charlotte, North Carolina. They've demonstrated their willingness to tackle this tough topic head-on. At one particular weekend service, for example, they addressed "The Lie and the Lure of Legalism." This is one of those messages that every church and every Christ-follower needs to hear.

I believe God designed Christianity to be about compassion and not condemnation. Fortunately there are more and more churches that have learned the importance of valuing this in their ministry as well. Mecklenburg Community Church is one of those ministries.

SETH GODIN
FIVE QUESTIONS

BACKSTORY—Seth is an author and speaker. He is responsible for many words in the marketer's vocabulary, including permission marketing, ideaviruses, purple cows, the dip, and sneezers. For more of his thoughts, check out his books *Small Is the New Big* and *Meatball Sundae*. Or you can catch him daily on his blog at sethgodin.typepad.com.

TONY: Seen any new "purple cows" that we should know about?

SETH: Actually, we're seeing more every single day. Which means that the bar is being raised, that it's harder than it was to do something people are willing to take a minute or two to check out.

TONY: What's a recent learning that has rocked your world?

SETH: The number of books read every year by the average adult in the United States is less than two. *Less than two!* So where is our information coming from? Does it matter that people don't read books or newspapers anymore?

TONY: What's your favorite blog to follow?

SETH: I follow ideas more than blogs.

TONY: Do you think marketing should be important for churches?

SETH: Nearly everyone who markets something suffers from this conceit: other people do marketing, but my product is so amazing and magical and important that marketing isn't necessary. Nowhere is this idea easier to embrace than in a church. After all, marketing seems contrived or selfish or callous. If you really and truly believe that your faith is the one and only right faith, how dare you market! But I don't think the "one and only right faith" is accurate. No one is particularly chosen or blessed or better. A look at history makes that really clear. So you need to get over that if you're going to grow. Yes, if you want to grow, you need to market.

TONY: What's one small thought from your book *Small Is the New Big* that could make a big impact for church leaders?

SETH: I have no business at all telling church leaders much of anything. I hope they'll find a nugget that resonates, especially if their goal is to spread kindness and openness. We need more of that.

SHOULD CHURCHES BUILD?

Outreach magazine published an interesting article by Thom Rainer, a researcher and current president of LifeWay Christian Resources. In the article, Rainer summarized some research addressing whether or not churches should continue to pursue building programs.

He acknowledged the debate that the American church continues to spend billions of dollars on new construction, yet there still remain very few healthy churches. The conclusion, without research, might suggest churches are wasting their money on new facilities when they could be using those dollars for other ministry efforts.

Rather than just relying on gut instinct, Rainer set out to research churches across the country. His team spoke to nearly a thousand church leaders in 321 churches. Fifty-eight of these interviews included on-site visits. Among his many findings: "We learned that 8 out of 10 churches experienced growth after a building program." Rainer's conclusion was this: "While a building program cannot make an unhealthy church healthy, it can equip and inspire healthy churches to become healthier. Our research concluded that church building programs tend to help, not hurt churches."[44]

That has been the experience at the churches where I've

served as well. We've been through a variety of different building phases, and we've experienced growth after each phase—both in attendance and spiritual steps.

Building programs aren't right for every church. But for the communities we're trying to reach, the facility matters. Building phases can encourage churches to become healthier by helping folks unify behind a vision, while creating additional space for people to hear the good news of Jesus Christ.

SINK YOUR SERMON SERIES

Scoping out what other churches across the country are doing to help people meet Jesus and take steps in their faith is one of my favorite things to do. By doing this over the past several years, I've learned that many churches use sermon series to both hone their message and encourage people to invite their friends, not just for one week but perhaps four or six. I've also noticed, however, that some churches implement sermon series much more effectively than others. And some series inherently engage the unchurched better than others.

Ironically, you can learn how to do things right from the churches who are doing it wrong. Here are:

✦ ✦ 10 WAYS TO SINK YOUR SERMON SERIES ✦ ✦

1. *Address questions that no one is asking.* Typically we have people's attention for thirty to forty-five minutes each week. So weigh what you really want people to know, and respond to the questions people are really asking. This requires first *knowing* the

TONY MORGAN

questions they're asking. For example, How do I raise my kids? How can I save my marriage? What am I supposed to do with my life?

2. *Schedule your series to last more than six weeks.* A series will probably lose momentum after six weeks. People consider a new series as an opportunity to invite their friends, but the longer the series drags on, the less likely those they invite will come.

3. *Pack your church calendar so full that inviting friends to worship isn't a priority.* The more activities and ministries you provide—not to mention the number of meetings you schedule—the less you'll focus on your weekend services. Ask yourself: What is our primary way for reaching people who don't attend church? If the answer is your weekend service, focus on making that as effective as possible by doing less of something else.

4. *Teach too much in each message.* Too many points can confuse not only your listeners but you as well. Pick one point and stick to it. And remember, brevity is your friend.

5. *Teach the truth without life application.* For the most part, people don't need more knowledge but rather to learn how to put their existing knowledge into action. They know Jesus died for them, but what does this mean for them when their alarm goes off on Monday morning?

6. *Assume the message stands alone.* The artistic and worship elements that surround the message need

to prepare people's hearts and minds for God's Word. People must hear the message, but they also need to experience it with their emotions.

7. *Don't tease the coming series with appropriate promotions.* Launching a series without letting people know it's coming does no good. How will your members invite people ahead of time? Promote what you'll be talking about and why they should care enough to attend.

8. *Don't creatively connect biblical truth with the spiritual conversations in our culture.* The Bible has a lot to say on hot topics in today's culture. And when culture lobs us a softball and opens up a spiritual dialogue, we should be ready to swing the bat.

9. *Make sure your series only connects with people who already attend your church.* Want to ignore the unchurched in your community? A surefire way to do this is to preach a sermon series that assumes your listeners are already Christians. Churches will eventually die when they stop focusing on people outside the congregation.

10. *Don't sweat the details.* A good series involves more than just developing a message. When a team of experts comes together to plan it all out—the art elements, the promotions, and the rest of the service experience—there's a much better chance the series will succeed in both offering biblical truth and reaching more people for Christ.[45]

TONY MORGAN

SKIN

I just took a personality profile. Our entire leadership team is doing it. We're using an assessment tool called "Leading from Your Strengths" that's available at ministryinsights.com. No real surprises. As much as I hate to admit it, the results were pretty accurate.

One of the statements that caught my attention was found in the section that outlined the suggested strategies for others when they're communicating with *me*. It included recommendations like, "Be prepared with facts and figures." And, "Respect his quiet demeanor." But the one that caught my attention was, "Keep at least three feet away from him."

That's when I wondered if the personality profile company had been secretly stalking me for the last number of years. Let's just say this statement confirmed that the profile is very accurate.

I put up with it. But I'm not a big fan of physical touch (well, with one exception). I know other people need physical touch, so I try to offer that in appropriate ways. But quite frankly, I kind of liken it to eating spinach. I know it's good for me and others, and I have to force myself to do it.

If you don't believe me, there are people out there who have stories they can share about my aversion to physical contact. I remember one particular incident involving my friend Corey Mann (mynameiscorey.com). I don't know what possessed him but, in a crowd of people at a hot tub, Corey tried to get a little too close—well within three feet. I made it clear to him that he shouldn't get any closer and exclaimed, "Whatever you do, don't touch my skin!" The way

I remember the story is that Corey cowered at that moment and retreated. Any other version that you hear of this incident is purely folklore.

Needless to say, God has wired each of us uniquely. There's a reason why he described us using the various parts of the human body (1 Cor. 12) to distinguish how we are all different and yet all needed for the body of Christ to live and grow.

Do you know how the other members of your team are wired? Do you know how to best communicate with them? Do you know what types of responsibilities most energize them? Do you know the functions that tend to drain them? Do you know whether or not you need to stay three feet away from them? If not, I recommend you consider using a profile assessment to begin a conversation with your teammates. No, they aren't one hundred percent accurate, but they do tend to reveal the uniqueness of who we are. Having that knowledge, if applied appropriately, can help a team function at a higher level.

That said, my position still stands. I'll give you a manly, side-shoulder hug if I have to, but *please*—don't touch my skin!

SONG

Lee and RoseAngela, two of our worship leaders at NewSpring, wrote a song that was used in one of our services. Great song. I was curious, though, to know more about their creative process. Did RoseAngela sit down at the piano and the song just sort of came to her? Did Lee get inspired when he was singing in the shower? Maybe one of them went out to dinner and ended up writing the lyrics on a napkin? Lee knows his Bible. Did God give him the song during one of his daily devotional times? I asked Lee about it.

Turns out our worship leaders actually schedule time to write music. This song came out of one of those sessions. Lee and RoseAngela planned to write that song. It was a good reminder to me that creativity rarely sneaks up on us.

- It usually involves practicing for years to hone our skills.
- It typically includes other people.
- Most times we actually have to discipline our lives to set aside time to create.
- It almost always involves hard work.
- Usually you have to create and fail many times before you find success.

No, I don't believe everyone has the gift that Lee and RoseAngela have. I do, however, believe each of us can be creative. We were created in God's image. God is creative. I believe God designed us to be creative as well. What if you're the person who's supposed to create that song, that book, that picture, that invention, that strategy? Are you disciplining your life to see that happen? Do you have a song?

SPAMMERS

Is it just me, or are all spammers poor spellers? Come on. Get with the program. Is it "shear" or "share"? I don't care if you're Nigerian and your dead uncle needs my checking account number to deposit $12 million—it's no excuse to not use spell-check.

I think it's about time someone led the charge to improve the quality of spam. If these folks are going to add noise to my life, then they should at least do it with excellence.

SPEEDY CHECKOUT

Emily and I ran into the store the other night to pick up a few items. Out of convenience, we stopped at the store that was on our way home. I normally shop at Target. I know. I pay a little more, but I get better help, a cleaner store, better quality products, and I don't ever have to wait in the queue (that's for all my British friends) to give someone my money.

I have a picture of Emily in the "speedy checkout" aisle at Wal-Mart. She's standing there holding the diapers, tennis balls, and knee pads we were more than ready to buy. (Bet you've never purchased that combination of products in one shopping trip.) Yet in the background, you can see that the vast majority of cash registers are not open. This situation screams, "We want your money, but we don't care about your time."

Experiences like this frustrate me, but they also cause me to consider what we may or may not be communicating to the guests at our church. I want people to hear about Jesus. Because of that, I don't want anything else we do to create a barrier for people to hear that message. Frankly, these are the issues that any church of any size can also easily address.

Isn't it amazing what goes through your mind while you stand in the "speedy checkout" aisle? If you think that's amazing, then you may want to know what goes through the minds of people who are visiting your church for the first time. Hopefully they're not taking pictures and writing books about it.

STAYING AWAKE

When people ask me why certain churches continue to experience growth, the one area that probably rises to the top is the quality teaching that happens week after week. There's power in God's Word. But I think you'd agree, not all communicators are created equal. Some are more gifted. Others are more experienced. That aside, I'm convinced there are specific strategies any communicator can use to improve the chances of their message being heard.

I took the time recently to figure out what it is (in my mind) that makes some folks more effective than others in their communications. This might not apply to anyone else, but I listed what really works for me. With that in mind, here are:

✦ ✦ 10 EASY WAYS TO KEEP ME AWAKE AND ENGAGED ✦ ✦ DURING AN ENTIRE MESSAGE

1. *Be real.* Let people see the actual human inside you. Most of the time, this will occur through your personal stories.
2. *Talk like normal people talk.* I didn't grow up in the church, so I don't understand when you talk with a Christian accent.

3. *Use humor.* If you don't make me laugh, I'm probably going to tune you out. By the way, the best humor is revealed through your everyday life.

4. *Don't tell me what to think.* Lead me on the journey toward truth, but let me reach my own conclusions. In other words, don't try to sell it.

5. *Be honest.* If I think you're credible, then there's a better chance I'll think your message is credible.

6. *Avoid being too polished.* In fact, I love it when you leave your prepared statements and share anything off the cuff.

7. *Reveal your weaknesses.* Silly as it seems, it makes me smile when I hear you tell about your mistakes. It helps me respect the areas where you *are* gifted.

8. *Be brief.* Shorter is better. I'm probably only going to remember one or, at the most, two things that you say.

9. *Make me smart.* I don't care how smart you are, but I like it when you make *me* feel smart. Simplify your statements and make it easy for me to apply what you're teaching.

10. *Tell me why I should care.* Help me understand why I should listen. If I'm not sure why what you're saying is relevant to my life, I'll be thinking about everything but your message.

I've never had a seminary course on preaching, so I really don't know anything about what it takes to prepare a good sermon. Hopefully this list will help you keep people alert and engaged in your message. It's not enough for folks to just hear what you're saying—the message really needs to impact their lives.

STEVEN FURTICK
ON KILLING COCKROACHES

BACKSTORY—Steven is the lead pastor of Elevation Church (elevationchurch.org) in Charlotte, North Carolina. Within two years of launching, Elevation was already seeing over 4,000 people attending services each weekend in two locations. Steven blogs at stevenfurtick.com.

I love the analogy of killing cockroaches. It's a very vivid picture of what we as leaders have to fight against every day. It creates a new, fresh way to speak about avoiding the tyranny of the urgent. "Killing cockroaches" communicates that for me.

Lately I have been teaching a principle to our staff about the difference between vision questions and decision questions. The goal is that my high level leaders would very rarely have to ask me questions about specific decisions. Instead they learn to come to me when they need clarification of the vision. My staff has open access to me to ask questions about the ultimate vision of our church, a specific project, or a new direction. To me, these questions are not cockroaches. Keeping clear answers to questions like these before my people at every new turn that we navigate as a leadership team will always be my responsibility. I can never delegate that to anyone else. If I find myself making decisions all day long, and if the questions revolve around decisions rather than vision, I haven't properly empowered my team or clarified my expectations. Or perhaps it's an indication that they are lacking capability to lead at a high level of execution.

This principle doesn't just apply to me. Recently in a job evaluation, I encouraged my executive pastor to limit the number of direct decisions he allowed himself to make on any given day. By doing this he forces the people who serve under his authority to make their own decisions, and he saves his best bandwidth as a leader for things that concern the greater vision.

STRAW HOUSE THINKING

Once upon a time in a far-off land, there lived a leader who supervised three little pigs. The leader was committed to excellence in his life and in his organization. He knew there was a direct correlation between the quality of the houses his pigs built and the success they had in protecting themselves from big, bad wolves.

The leader obsessed about every detail. He also made it clear to his team of pigs that they, too, needed to obsess about every little detail. It didn't take long for the pigs to realize that their interpretation of excellence might not be the same as their supervisor's perception of excellence. Because of that, the pigs began to bring every decision about every detail to the leader. The pigs didn't want to run the risk that they might not "get it right."

Over time the leader found himself in a challenging predicament. He was overwhelmed because he had to touch everything. And he was frustrated that he was responsible for generating every new idea. For example, he was the one who originally developed the design for straw houses. His pigs built excellent straw houses. In fact, no one built straw houses any better. What they did, they did well. But they were stuck.

"If you try to control things, that's self-limiting," said Michael Dell, chief executive officer of Dell. "The easiest way to think about this is that if all the decisions inside an organization had to roll up to the center of the company or to one person, it's a massive bottleneck to progress."[46]

In the end, the leader in this story learned that sometimes core values collide. His commitment to excellence wasn't the problem. Control was the problem. His obsession with getting it right became a roadblock to progress. He discovered the need to empower his team with broad responsibilities to fulfill the organization's mission while still holding them accountable to the overall vision and values. He needed to let the pigs take risks . . . and sometimes fail.

Our leader was very savvy. He identified the potential threat of a menacing wolf. Instead of telling the pigs the exact dimensions of the house they needed to build and the materials they needed to use, he learned that a smart leader empowers his little pigs to prepare for the next blowhard that knocks on their door. In the end, this gives the pigs freedom to design a strategy the leader may never have considered. That's where innovation and creativity are birthed.

That leader is me. It happened again yesterday. I jumped to "the answer" without giving my team the opportunity to discover a brand new solution. The moral of this story is this: If all I've known is straw houses and I control every detail of their construction, then my leadership will never generate brick house ideas.

STUPID LEADERSHIP MISTAKES

I recently celebrated my tenth year in ministry. Prior to that, I spent about ten years in the city management profession. Those milestones have provoked a lot of introspection in recent days. I've served under several great leaders. I also had, from a relatively early age, the opportunity to find myself in leadership roles, where I learned a lot about what it takes to be a leader. Honestly, though, the most significant lessons were learned through trial and error. And let me tell you, there have been quite a few mistakes along the way.

Someone recently asked me whether or not there are times when I knowingly let people make what I perceive to be a mistake in their ministry roles. This in itself may be another leadership error on my part, but I think there are instances when it is appropriate to let people try and fail. To do otherwise is to invite every detail of every decision to land in my lap. For leaders to be fully empowered and have the same opportunities I've had to grow, they, too, must experience what it is to sometimes make mistakes and respond to the consequences of those challenges.

That said, I've also tried to learn as much as I can from my mentors, training opportunities, and reading about leadership from those more experienced than I am. Fortunately, I've been able to avoid some mistakes by learning from the mistakes of others. With the hope that it may be the same for you, let me share what I believe to be the stupidest mistakes I've made in leadership. Granted, the mistakes I'm prone to make will look different from yours. Mine are certainly a reflection of the quirks (and sometimes sin) in my life. But hopefully by sharing a little of what I've learned, you can avoid these unfortunate miscues.

✦ ✦ 10 STUPIDEST LEADERSHIP ✦ ✦ MISTAKES I'VE MADE

1. *Hiring too fast and firing too slow.* When a position is open that you know needs to be filled and the right person isn't available, it's hard to wait. The tendency is to fill the role with the best available person, but sometimes that's not the *right* person. Let me just confirm that it's a lot easier to tell someone they're not a good fit for the job *before* you hire them than after you've brought them on the team. On the flip side, I've made the mistake of waiting too long to let someone go. I can remember one particular situation when I let a problem go for months without dealing with it head-on. It

was impacting me, my family, and the rest of the team. More importantly, I was getting in the way of God doing a work in this particular employee's life. I thought I was doing him a favor by keeping him on the team. The reality was that he needed to move on to experience all that God had for him.

2. *Trying to fix the problem rather than the process.* Not to be crass, but I've found it's a lot better to potty-train my kids than to continue changing messy diapers. Regrettably, though, there have been too many times in leadership roles when I've found myself reacting to a problem rather than addressing the process that prevents the situation from occurring in the first place. It takes a lot of discipline to rise above the emotion of a difficult situation and try to discern how a broken system needs to be fixed.

3. *Putting the projects before the people.* Others may have the opposite challenge of letting their love of people get in the way of actually accomplishing the purpose of the organization. But because I'm not naturally a people person, I tend to be too task-driven. Good leaders find the perfect balance between getting the job done and embracing the relational component of doing life as a team.

4. *Delegating tasks instead of responsibility.* When pushed into a corner, I naturally revert back to my perfectionist tendencies. I know in my mind the way it should be done. And if I let myself, I'll fall into

the trap of thinking I'm the only one who can get it done. First of all, I'm not that good. Someone else can usually do it better. Second, the failure to empower others with real responsibilities is a guaranteed recipe for limiting the potential of your ministry. This is the number one reason that most churches don't grow beyond a couple hundred people. In those situations the pastor will, at best, only delegate tasks. Real leadership development doesn't happen until an effort is made to build a team and give away ministry responsibility.

5. *Assuming it's always black and white.* Maybe it's all those years I spent in local government fulfilling my bureaucratic responsibilities. Or maybe it's just because following prescribed rules is easier than dealing with the mess of following God's lead and making wise decisions. The reality, of course, is that much of life isn't black and white. And I've found I'm chasing my tail if I think I'm going to be able to create policies or guidelines to address or prevent every situation that could potentially arise.

6. *Not following my gut.* Or is that the Holy Spirit? One of my spiritual gifts is discernment. But I've noticed that people's strengths can also lead to their biggest challenges. For me, discernment can lead to paralysis through analysis. When that happens, I tend to get in the way of what God is trying to accomplish. In an effort to make the best decision possible, I sometimes get stuck trying to acquire

information rather than seeking God's direction and taking action. Yes, we're called to plan and seek counsel. But that initial reaction you sense could very well be God's prompting.

7. *Dwelling on the worst-case scenario.* Again, this is what happens when I let my focus wander from God to the circumstances around me. It's appropriate to plan and take steps to prevent those bad situations from occurring. It's sin when this turns into worry. It's really kind of humorous to see the stupid mistakes we can make when we begin to think we're in control. I've wasted way too much time worrying about ministry challenges that never happened.

8. *Waiting until there's a problem to provide feedback.* I really do hate this about myself, and I'm consciously trying to improve with God's help. But to be quite truthful, I'm encouragement-challenged. Like I mentioned before, I've always had this strong sense of what the end product needs to look like. So one of my biggest mistakes as a leader has been withholding encouragement when the team delivers and only speaking up when expectations aren't met. I'm trying to improve, but I'm not there yet.

9. *Staying busy.* I've fallen into this trap too many times. In my mind I tell myself that if I'm busy, then I'm adding value. The reality is that our busyness can get in the way of effectiveness. We can be busy about the wrong things. And if we don't discipline our lives, we'll find ourselves investing a lot of time

TONY MORGAN

with little impact. E-mail is one example of this trap for me. If I wanted to, I could spend the entire day processing e-mail and not really accomplishing anything. That's why when I plan my week, I actually plan the times when I'm going to respond to e-mail messages.

10. *Spending too much time on the details rather than the dreams.* This is a natural corollary to the mistake of staying busy. When life gets busy and I get invested in all the dirty details flowing my way, I lose site of the dreams that God has for me. Here's the reality: those dreams usually come when the pace of my life slows enough to do stuff like read, pray, rest, experience new places, and meet new people. Dealing with the dailiness of life doesn't allow for that. It needs to be planned and prioritized. We need to create space to experience God and all that he has for us.

Those are my biggest mistakes. I wish I had the space to share more stories behind them. All I can say is that God is gracious to allow me the opportunity to continue to live and learn what it means to be a leader. My journey isn't complete. Yours isn't either. And I hope this list encourages you to consider where God is growing you in your leadership role. He loves you too much to leave you where you are today. Your influence is too important to the lives of those around you. I'm thankful that God is in a continual process of redeeming us for his glory and his purposes.

SUPERCOOL?

Not too long ago, I saw an article in *Advertising Age* talking about Wal-Mart's less than effective attempt to reconnect with teenagers. Wal-Mart tried to develop a Web site similar to MySpace that encouraged teens to create their own page and submit videos. The teens were competing for the chance to have their videos used in Wal-Mart commercials. As the article points out, "The site is an attempt at closing the trend gap Wal-Mart now faces as Target wins more teen-apparel dollars."

Only problem is that teenagers are seeing right through this attempt to be hip. For example, one of the students interviewed in the article explained, "Some of the kids looked like they were trying to be supercool, but they weren't at all, and they were just being kind of weird," she said. "Are these real kids?"[47]

This brings me to the conversation about better blogging or better teaching or better worship leading or better marketing or better Web design. You have to be you. You can't try to be something you're not. The people you're trying to reach will see right through it.

While we're on the topic of MySpace, I find this to be an interesting phenomenon. Why is it that the same teens who complain about a lack of authenticity in today's institutions and leadership also have their own MySpace pages where they're pretending to be someone they're not? Who will choose to be real?

TONY MORGAN

SYSTEMS BREED INNOVATION

I was recently having dinner with a group of friends at a conference. One of the women at the table shared a story about a church she had been communicating with in recent months. Her business was trying to assist the church with some services. She said it took the church a full year to consider their proposal. The process involved meetings with five separate committees, a vote by the deacon board with over forty members, and a vote from the full congregation. This church has so many committees, there is actually a committee of the committees to track all the committees. Is it any wonder that some churches aren't experiencing fruit from their ministry? Too many people are spending too much time in meetings rather than in meaningful ministry. With horror stories like this in mind, I understand why pastors and other leaders would want to avoid establishing systems and guidelines for their churches. Why would a growing, vibrant church want to create systems and policies? Bureaucracy—bad. Loosey-goosey—good. If we don't have guidelines in place, that means less red tape and more freedom to do what we need to do to make our ministry great, right? Fewer systems mean more innovation—or do they?

Generally I would agree that having too many policies or the wrong policies would certainly stifle ministry effectiveness. But at the same time, I've seen how a lack of systems or poor systems can limit ministry effectiveness. As churches grow, they need to move from a purely entrepreneurial approach to one that also values the development of effective systems and strategies in areas like staffing, technology, building scheduling, and finances. And more important, appropriate systems and strategies also help people take steps in their faith journey by helping them connect in relationships, ministry, and membership in the church. Through systems, big churches remain small enough to personalize the experience for every attendee.

Without systems and strategies, all decisions rise to the top of the organization. Can I make that purchase? Can I hire that person? Can I start a new group? Can I connect with that ministry team? Can I use that room? Without systems, all of these decisions rise to the top of the ministry. That'll work for a while, but then that one person or committee or board will be overwhelmed. People will get frustrated. Ministry will have to pause until more direction is provided. That's when churches plateau or decline.

The right systems and structure, however, can actually *benefit* ministry and free people to lead and to innovate while still providing appropriate accountability and responsibility. Here are some simple thoughts to hopefully help you move in the right direction:

- *Be ruthless about creating new rules.* Always ask: Is there a way we can accomplish this without creating a policy?
- *Whenever you create a new guideline, ask: Will this make life easier for our team?* Good systems remove obstacles and free people to accomplish ministry without waiting for decisions.

- *Are people meeting to strategize and accomplish ministry, or are they meeting to allocate resources?* Resource allocation involves power, and it's easier than doing ministry or talking about the big picture. The fact is, systems and guidelines can easily be established to allocate money, time, and space without committees having to gather for a vote.

- *Are people meeting to decide something because a leader hasn't been empowered to make the decision?* It doesn't take a committee to select a paint color. Those are decisions that can be delegated to one volunteer or staff member who knows the color trends for what will be warm and bright with a touch of sophistication and luxury. (I think that means Harvest Gold is back!)

- *Do you really need that committee?* At NewSpring, we only have one lay board. Everyone else is serving on a team that's doing ministry. Ask people if they really enjoy and have time for another meeting. I'm pretty confident you won't find a groundswell of support for more meetings.

Empower staff and volunteers. Give people freedom to lead within a framework that provides appropriate accountability and identifies responsibility. That freedom will benefit your ministry by encouraging people to actively engage in ministry while allowing them to innovate and create. That's why growing churches need to be as committed to effective systems as they are to embracing innovation.

TABLE CONVERSATIONS

We were sitting around the table eating breakfast this morning when, I'm not sure how, the word "reconciliation" came up in our conversation. Emily tried to put that big word into smaller words that the kids might understand. "It's kind of like when one person admits they did something wrong and the other person forgives them. They've reconciled."

I was incensed. Why didn't she quote 2 Corinthians 5:20? "Now then we are ambassadors for Christ, as though God did beseech you by us: we pray you in Christ's stead, be ye reconciled to God" (KJV). Then Jacob mentioned that the word "reconciliation" is in one of the Christmas carols. "Peace on earth and mercy mild—God and sinners reconciled."

Trying to explain biblical truth using familiar songs? That's heresy. Oh wait, that's a hymn, so it's acceptable. Or maybe it isn't. The words to the hymn, written by Charles Wesley, were put together with a melody not intended for sacred music that was written by Felix Mendelssohn—who also wrote quite a bit of "secular" music that's closely associated with Victorian culture. Does that make it a Christian song, or a secular song? (Life was so much easier before Amy Grant crossed over to pop music.) Why didn't Jacob just quote Hebrews 2:17? "Wherefore in all things it behoved him to be made like unto his brethren, that he might be a merciful and faithful high priest in things pertaining to God, to make reconciliation for the sins of the people" (KJV).

Then Emily tried to explain, of all things, how we reconcile our checkbook every month—making sure our balance and the balance the bank statement indicates are in harmony.

TONY MORGAN

What does she think she's doing? People don't need to hear personal stories about how biblical doctrine applies to everyday life. They need to hear Leviticus 8:15—"And he slew it; and Moses took the blood, and put it upon the horns of the altar round about with his finger, and purified the altar, and poured the blood at the bottom of the altar, and sanctified it, to make reconciliation upon it" (KJV).

Or maybe one of the kids could have offered a Spurgeon quote on reconciliation. That, of course, is also acceptable.

I hate it when my family waters down the Word of God.

TALENT

I was enjoying a quick nine holes with a good friend of mine this evening. We got on the topic of finding good talent. His company is hiring several people right now. He talked about the challenges of finding the right people for the right roles.

It was probably a ploy to get me to play stinky golf (which I did) because I started thinking about the talent that surrounds me on a daily basis. This is how it works. Every time you have the chance, you hire the most talented person you can find who loves Jesus and the church. You give them the freedom to do their best every day. Then several years later, you wake up and realize: everyone around me is far more talented than I am. You recognize the fact that it's only by God's grace that they still pay you to show up every day.

Now do me a favor. Please keep this a secret. Don't let my boss know what's up. He still thinks I'm actually adding value to the ministry. It's a charade. Every once in a while, I try to razzle-dazzle him to divert his attention. The reality, of course, is that my team surpassed me years ago. I'm just along for the ride now. It's a pretty fun ride.

Oh, I lost by five strokes. I hate playing stinky golf.

TASTES LIKE GRITS

Since moving to South Carolina, I've become quite a connoisseur of Southern culture. But one thing I can't acquire a taste for is country music. If I did, however, here are:

✦ ✦ 10 COUNTRY SONGS I'D WRITE ✦ ✦
IF I LIKED COUNTRY MUSIC

1. She Thinks My Audi's Sexy
2. Ladies Love Country Boys with Midwestern Accents
3. You, Me, and a Glass of Sweet Tea
4. Get Drunk and Be Somebody, Unless You're Baptist
5. Wake Me Up When There's a Wreck (The NASCAR Ballad)
6. Snoot Shootin' Boogers
7. Jesus, Take the Wheel 'Cause There's a Smokey on My Tail
8. Feels Like Love but Tastes Like Grits
9. Cowboy, Take the Dixie Chicks Away
10. I'll Listen to Country Music When the Waffle House Decides to Close

TONY MORGAN

TELL ME YOUR STORY

When's the last time you listened—really listened—to another person's painful story? For me, hearing stories of the real pain in others' lives increases my sense of urgency. It helps me realize there's no such thing as "normal." It forces me to become more intentional about how I interact with people. It reminds me there's a search for healing, forgiveness, and hope going on all around me. As Christians, we know that the answer to sin problems is Jesus. But many people are searching for something other than "truth." They're not ready to hear that yet. Their pain consumes them.

Knowing that stories of pain are walking through the doors of our sanctuary each Sunday should cause us to revisit what we preach and how we preach it. I'm reminded of an interesting interaction Jesus had with a person caught in sin. Initially he didn't address the person's sin. His first priority was to address the accusers. Jesus showed compassion to the sinner. He didn't *condemn* the sinner but he did, however, redirect the sinner. At your church, are you simultaneously showing compassion and helping point people in a new direction?

Most of us have work to do in this area. Consider these questions to help you design a ministry strategy that meets people where they are—in the midst of their painful stories.

- Are you willing to be vulnerable in your messages, sharing the imperfections and challenges you face?
- When you teach about sin, do you also teach about hope? Do people leave condemned, or do they leave encouraged to take their next step?

- Do people have an opportunity to share their stories, no matter how painful they might be?
- Are you creating opportunities for hurting people to connect in a community where they can find support and healing?

We serve a God who called us to go to the lost. Care for the sick. Touch the untouchables. But too often we fail to see the painful stories that hide behind seemingly normal lives. Are you prepared to listen and help?[48]

THAT'S MY SON!

Someone gave me the kindest compliment today, and they were actually talking about my son. One of our good friends that we've met through youth sports had this to say about him: "We will surely miss Jacob. He's a great kid. His passion, leadership, and intelligence are amazing to watch."

You need to know that Jacob is a great little athlete. (In other words, my son could kick your son's butt on the basketball court or the baseball diamond.) What encouraged me about this message was that Jacob's athletic skills were not acknowledged—it was everything else Jacob demonstrates in his character. What our friend shared is true. That's who Jacob is—on and off the court. I'm so proud of him.

As a proud dad, it made me wonder how God reacts to our conversations—you know, how we treat each other. I wonder what God thinks when he hears comments like this about his children. I bet it makes him smile as well.

TONY MORGAN

This was just a reminder for me to be wise about how I talk about fellow Christ followers.

TRANSITION VS. CHANGE

I get many questions from people who are interested in knowing how they can transition their ministries. Those are challenging questions for me because I've never really faced that situation in the ministries I've helped to lead. Both churches I worked for were still under the leadership of their founding pastors. Because of that, I know that my experience is very different from the experiences that other, more established churches share.

With that in mind, I thought I'd get the perspective of a good friend who has led his church through a significant transition. Scott Hodge is the lead pastor of The Orchard Church Community (orchardvalleyonline.com) in Aurora, Illinois. This is what Scott had to share:

> First of all, I think it's important that pastors and church leaders understand the difference between change and transition. Change has more to do with adjusting the "externals" of our churches. That includes things like church name, musical style, teaching style, etc. For us, those were the easy things to change. (I'll explain why in a minute.) Thankfully too, in our situation, we didn't have a lot of "red tape" or multilevels of bureaucracy to wade through when it came time to make these changes.

Transition is the tough part. While change focuses on the externals of the organization, transition has to do with changing the internal culture or DNA of the church (i.e., people's hearts and mind-sets). Not only is this extremely challenging, but it is costly! Which is why, I think, so many pastors are afraid to go all the way in their journey of change.

Let me get biblical for a second. What I think tends to happen over and over again for so many pastors is instead of pouring new wine into new wineskins, they end up wasting tons of time, energy, and resources pouring new wine into old wineskins. So even though lots of changes have been made, things feel the same under that thin surface of change. (It might look shiny on the outside, but the inside smells like the old.)

I'm convinced that the reason The Orchard's culture looks completely different now than it did five years ago is because of multiple tough decisions that were made up front and the willingness of our leaders to pay the high price for the new wineskins.

And let me tell you—it cost us a ton! It cost us people, which of course led to the loss of financial resources, which in turn led to almost losing everything except our determination and focus on what we believed God had called us to do. But I kid you not, there were multiple weeks when we wondered if that coming weekend would be our last together as a church.

TONY MORGAN

Five years later, we have seen an over 200 percent increase in our weekend attendance, a 180-degree turn in our culture/DNA, and best of all, we are seeing God changing lives in ways we would have never imagined. It is truly the most humbling thing I have ever experienced in my entire life.

By the way, William Bridges does a fantastic job explaining the difference between "change" and "transition" in his book *Managing Transitions.*

Read more about Scott and his ministry, The Orchard, by following his blog at scotthodge.org.

TROY GRAMLING
ON KILLING COCKROACHES

BACKSTORY—Troy is the lead pastor of Flamingo Road Church (flamingoroad.org) in Cooper City, Florida. Theirs is a multisite ministry with six campuses including their Internet campus. You can follow Troy's life and ministry at troyandsteph.com.

TONY: Tell me about an instance when you found yourself "killing cockroaches."

TROY: A leadership challenge for a growing organization is that what once was a legitimate task can become "killing cockroaches." The cockroach I often run to kill is problem solving. Once upon a time, it was my problem to figure out our parking lot strategy for big days; it no longer is. While I used to spend hours with the student pastor to devise a strategy that will reach students, I no longer sit with him. While I was the go-to guy for determining a plan of action for a disgruntled parishioner, I'm no longer on that front line. Now when I get involved in parking lot strategy, student ministry development, or disgruntled parishioners, I am killing cockroaches. What once was my responsibility is now a cockroach.

TONY: What are some of the strategies you've implemented to avoid it?

TROY: Hiring the Orkin man. When the church was small, it meant subcontracting things that I could do for free. For example, I could have run our first stewardship campaign, but the time required to crawl around in the dark with my shoe trying to find the cockroach wasn't cost-effective or inspiring to the team. But when I subcontracted the systems and administration of the campaign to the "Orkin Man" of stewardship campaigns, I was able to focus on the task that I was better equipped to do. So today, whenever I hear that familiar scream of a cockroach sighting, I reach for my Rolodex (which is conveniently located in my iPhone) instead of my shoe. I've discovered there are many volunteers who are better equipped and more effective at certain tasks than I am, though I admit, there are times I miss the "congrats" that come with being the all-powerful cockroach killer.

TONY MORGAN

TONY: What have you learned from some of these experiences?

TROY: If we come running, people will keep screaming. It may start with one cockroach, but it will then progress to an army of them. That's why I no longer get disheartened by the staff's looks of confusion when I purchase cans of cockroach spray for them.

TONY: How do you help your team avoid "killing cockroaches"?

TROY: By reminding them that people go to school to study how to kill cockroaches. When we impose on that, we keep people from reaching their God-given potential. Just a few days ago we had an exterminator at our house. I was amazed at the passion and excitement he had for what I just see as a pest. If our team sees me killing a cockroach in their office, they will do the same. If they see me training and equipping them to kill cockroaches, they will go and do likewise. The most effective way for me to model this is to remove my cockroach-killing crown I worked hard for and pass it on to others with the admonition to wear it lightly and be ready to pass it on too.

TURN RIGHT

On our way back from the beach one time, we came to the intersection pictured on the following page.

I was heading north. As you'll notice on closer inspection, I had four options for going north, including the opportunity

to go left, go straight, or turn right. Fortunately for me, the navigation system did the work for me. I wasn't looking for options. I just wanted someone to tell me to turn right.

A few years ago, a Columbia University professor completed a series of studies that resulted in an article "When Choice Is Demotivating: Can One Desire Too Much of a Good Thing?"[49] In one experiment, they set up a tasting booth at a grocery store. They offered twenty-four different exotic flavors of jams for people to taste in one instance. In a separate instance, they only offered six varieties. Customers who stopped by the booth received a coupon for one dollar off the purchase of a jar. Here are some of the results from this experiment:

- More people stopped at the booth that offered more choices; however, folks tasted the same number of jams in both locations.
- More importantly, 30 percent of the people with a choice of six jams actually purchased a jar. Only three percent of the people with a choice of twenty-four jams made a purchase. Fewer choices generated more purchases.

Barry Schwartz wrote in his book *The Paradox of Choice:* "When people have no choice, life is almost unbearable. As the number of available choices increases, as it has in our consumer culture, the autonomy, control, and liberation this variety brings are powerful and positive. But as the number of choices keeps growing, negative aspects of having a multitude of options begin to appear. As the number of choices grows further, the negatives escalate until we become overloaded. At this point, choice no longer liberates, but debilitates."[50]

Now take a look around your ministry. How many choices do people have for participating in a service, event, class, program, etc.? How many options do people have for selecting a ministry? Our instinct tells us that if we offer more options, more people will respond and take a step in their spiritual journey. In reality, we may be making life more difficult for people who are looking for a clear path for where they should go next. It may be time to eliminate all the options for going north and just encourage people to turn right.

UNFILTERED FEEDBACK

I love listening to children. They don't sugarcoat anything. You get to hear everything that's on their mind—unfiltered. Because of that, they are willing to say what everyone else is thinking. Bruce Johnson (brucedjohnson.com) shared about this type of scenario. This is how he described his story:

"After visiting [this one church] I asked [my child] what they thought of this church. [This child] said, "Well, once I get used to being bored, I'll be OK." Isn't that an amazing statement? Already by a young age, this child had come to the conclusion that if they were going to go to church, they had better get used to the idea of church being boring."[51]

I grew up in an irrelevant, boring church. This might sound trivial to you, but one of the reasons we started attending Granger Community Church back in 1998 was because we didn't want our kids growing up thinking that church is irrelevant and boring. Granger has committed millions of dollars and hundreds of staff members and volunteers to ministry for kids—over a thousand of them every weekend. Some might argue that time and money could have been invested elsewhere. Speaking as a parent of four kids who now *love* going to church, I'm convinced otherwise.

Church shouldn't be boring. To prevent this from happening, it means committing yourself to an age-appropriate ministry strategy for every generation in the church. My kind of church doesn't look like my kids' kind of church. Even church done well can be boring if we don't target our message and communicate it effectively to the audiences we're trying to reach.

TONY MORGAN

VALUES

A couple of months ago, I did an exercise with my team to make sure that my words and actions were communicating what I really valued. I had two groups from my team answer the question: "What do I really value as we do ministry life together?"

After the two lists were compiled, I asked both teams to identify the highest values. I suggested it might help them to identify times when I've been frustrated about something and consider what value was being challenged. Through that process they identified:

- being honest and sharing opinions
- protecting the unity and trust within our team
- excellence
- leveraging volunteer teams (leading, not doing)

A couple of realizations came out of this exercise for me. First, it was affirming that the teams identified and prioritized the things I really value. Second, I realized there are certain freedoms I give up because I've built a team that embraces these values. For example:

- *I've given up the freedom to make decisions on the direction of our/my ministry without input from my team.* I've hired a bunch of people who have opinions and aren't afraid to share them. If I don't allow them to express that part of who they are, they will feel undervalued and unfulfilled.

- *I've given up the freedom to remain disconnected.* I've hired a team that expects full integration of my private life, my family life, and my ministry life. In order for them to have trust in me, they have to know me and know that I know them. This means I have to fight every bit of my introvert tendencies to remain fully engaged in their lives and to reveal what's happening in my life.
- *I've given up the freedom to coast.* I've hired a team of recovering perfectionists. They're driven. They're big dreamers. They have high standards of excellence. That means I can't slack off. I have to pull my share of the load. I can't let the team down.
- *I've given up the freedom to do it myself.* I've hired a team that wants to empower others. They under-stand the value of giving ministry away. This means I can't hold on to everything I'm doing today—even if it feels like I can do it better. It's harder to build teams to accomplish ministry, but the ministry is far healthier in the long run when I let go.

So what are *your* leadership values? Does your team know what you value? Do they experience it daily? Maybe it's time you asked them.

VENDING MACHINE

I had a great conversation with some friends a few days ago. One of the women was talking about her old job. She left that position to pursue her dream. I don't remember what she used to do, but they replaced her old position with a vending machine. I'm glad she left her job. She was designed for so much more.

- How are you investing your life?
- Is it what you were designed to do?
- Are you fulfilled?
- Do you enjoy the people around you? Do they bring out the best in you? Do you bring out the best in them?
- Do you have enough financial resources to contribute to God's work and support your family?
- What lasting impact are you making?

Life is short. Just wanted to make sure you realized that sometimes you have to make the move. Sometimes God doesn't fully reveal his will until you take the first step (Josh. 3:14–17). Live boldly.

VENTI GOD

One of my teammates passed along an interesting article from a recent issue of *Psychology Today*. The article talks about the rapid growth of Starbucks and (among other things) attributes its growth to the "Starbucks experience" rather than the coffee. Here are some highlights from the article and the questions and thoughts it raised in my mind:

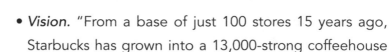

- *Vision.* "From a base of just 100 stores 15 years ago, Starbucks has grown into a 13,000-strong coffeehouse armada. It operates cafes in all 50 states and in 37 countries. . . . The company now opens more than 2,000 coffeehouses per year, an average of six new stores a day."[52] The company's current goal is to have 40,000 stores worldwide. Does anyone else read that and think our vision for the church pales in comparison? We complain about and try to discredit the ministry of churches that are approaching 40,000 people while this company (that's just trying to sell more coffee) is trying to open 40,000 unique locations. Aren't we thinking too small?

- *Intentionality.* "At Starbucks, nothing is accidental. Everything the customer interacts with, from the obsessively monitored store environment down to the white paper cups, is the product of deliberation and psychological research. The coffeehouse as we know it is a calculated creation." It ticks me off that the church embraces a passive (or maybe it's just lazy) approach to spreading the gospel while Starbucks has demonstrated this much intentionality in selling coffee.

- *Community.* "Starbucks filled America's need for a public gathering spot—a 'third place,' with home and work being place one and two. This became Starbucks' community rallying cry: It wasn't a coffee company, but a place for bringing people together through the social glue of coffee." Here's an example of a need that people had that could have easily been filled by the church. Maybe we're too focused on arguing about what we're against instead of being what the church was intended to be in people's lives.

TONY MORGAN

207

- *Atmosphere.* Starbucks interviewed coffee drinkers and found that they "talked very little about the coffee itself, but quite a bit about feelings and atmosphere. . . . The coffee wasn't the point—the feel of the place was." Here's the reality—Starbucks just wants to sell more coffee. But we don't hear blogging baristas complaining about how Starbucks has watered down the coffee because they're actually paying attention to people's feelings and the atmosphere of their stores.

What if God gifted artists to create an atmosphere for people to be more receptive to hearing the gospel? What if God created some people with the gift of hospitality to design a welcoming environment for people to hear the gospel? What if God gifts people and directs them through the Holy Spirit to think about effective building design, sound systems, video capabilities, and children's ministry so that more people might hear the gospel? Is it possible that we're trying to put God in a box by limiting how he chooses to reach people?

I happen to believe that God will use methods we haven't even seen before to reach people who have yet to commit their lives to Christ. As I read through the Bible again, I'm amazed at the variety of different approaches God uses to get people's attention and transform lives. I don't think he's done creating. And I don't think he's done redeeming people's lives.

VISION

A few random thoughts on vision:

- Vision is easy when you launch.

- Vision is what distinguishes one organization from the next. Both may be great organizations. They just have unique visions.

- If you grow, then eventually someone will try to shift the vision in a different direction. That's a guarantee.

- People need to be reminded frequently of what the vision is and where you're going next.

- Sometimes you have to confront people's agenda when it's not in line with the vision. Doesn't necessarily mean their agenda is wrong. Just means it's not *your* vision.

- Sometimes you have to ask a leader to step down if they can't fully support the vision. Doesn't mean they're not a good leader. Just means they're not *your* leader.

- Vision challenges can rock smaller organizations and go almost unnoticed in larger organizations.

- There's more vision stability in a larger organization but also more opportunity for complacency.

- The vision needs to be big enough to capture the hearts of leaders.

- The vision rarely changes, but the immediate objectives for accomplishing the vision must constantly be defined.

- The top positional leader has to be the loudest voice and the most passionate champion for the vision. That role can't be delegated.

- Vision unifies.

TONY MORGAN

WALKING ON WATER

A few days ago I walked on water. Not literally. I don't particularly like water. I didn't learn to swim until I married Emily. She broke swimming records growing up. I played golf. No, I didn't break any golf records, but I did frequently hit balls into the water. So I'm familiar with water. I just don't like to spend time in it . . . or on it.

This story began when I noticed my weedeater wasn't functioning properly. I was engaging the trigger to increase the throttle, but nothing was happening. So I shut off the engine, unscrewed the casing around the trigger, and found that it was broken. And unfortunately the throttle cable was connected to the plastic trigger. No amount of duct tape in the world was going to fix this problem. I was stuck.

You need to know—I'm not very mechanically inclined. OK, I'm not *at all* mechanically inclined. Both my parents were music majors. There aren't many mechanical repairs involved in music education. Because of that, I never really learned how to fix anything. Instead, I learned how to pay the fix-it people to fix things.

I don't know what prompted me, but I decided to tackle this repair on my own. I called the nice people at Sears and ordered the replacement part. After the part arrived, I started taking apart my weedeater. This was quite a moment. I don't normally step out of the boat like this.

At one point, my son walked by the garage and saw all the screws and weedeater parts strewn over the garage floor, and he couldn't believe what he was seeing. I can assure you that he had never seen anything like this before at our house.

For some reason, he's not impressed that I know how many sharps there are in the key of D. But seeing me hunched over a toolbox and various small-engine parts—*that* catches his attention.

Jacob was so surprised by the unlikely occurrence that he ran in to get Emily. A short time later, Emily came out to see what once was a weedeater. She smiled at me, shook her head, and returned inside. Remember, Emily is an expert swimmer. Because of that, she knows signs of drowning when she sees them.

This story, however, has a happy ending. After several attempts at reassembly, I was able to put the weedeater back together. I'm proud to say I accomplished this while making sure there weren't any leftover screws, and absolutely no duct tape was used. After laying hands on my weedeater and saying a brief but Spirit-filled prayer, I attempted to start the weedeater.

People say the first step out of the boat is the hardest. For me, I've found that when I feel like I'm drowning, the *next* step is always the hardest. It's pretty easy for me to turn around and get back in the boat. I don't like that about myself. I wish I could take steps of faith without fear. Then again, maybe it's the fear that leads me to faith. Either way, I'm trying to spend more time out on the water.

The weedeater started. The new trigger and throttle cable worked to perfection. I was able to whack a lot of weeds. You may read this and think, "Tony needs to get out more—people repair weedeaters every day." But Tony doesn't repair weedeaters every day. This was uncharted territory for me.

TONY MORGAN

I was cutting (or at least trimming) a completely new path. For one brief moment, I was walking on water.

Now if you'll excuse me. I need to Google "furnace maintenance." Sometime between now and the time I get home, I need to figure out how to replace the furnace filter. A handyman's work is never done.

WEB SITES: GOOD FOR NOTHING?

I own a Pontiac Montana minivan. I purchased it several years ago. I like my minivan. I've never gone on Pontiac's Web site since I've owned the minivan. I'm sure it has lots of helpful information to sell more minivans, but I don't care. I've already purchased mine.

My son plays little league baseball. My son loves baseball. The league has a Web site, but we still have to register in person at the beginning of each season. I've never been on the Web site. Neither has my son.

I'm a fan of the Cleveland Indians. I love the Tribe. The Indians have a Web site with all kinds of stories about how great the team is doing. I've never read the stories. The only time I've used the Web site is to purchase game tickets. I read about the Indians through my home page on My Yahoo.

I belong to an organization for leaders. I've belonged to the organization for several years. They have a Web site, but they're more committed to updating their magazine. I rarely read the magazine because I have leadership insights coming to me daily through RSS feeds. I never visit the organization's Web site. It just has content from their magazine.

I know an author. I used to read every book he published. That author has a Web site. He uses it to sell more books. I don't visit his Web site, but I do visit Seth's because he's always sharing fresh ideas with me—for free. I have to pay for the other author's ideas. I buy Seth's books now.

I used to have a checking account at a local bank. The bank has a Web site. In fact, the bank began offering online checking and bill payment to make banking easier for their customers. Only problem was they charged their customers more to use this service. I found a bank a few hours away that offered those same services for free. I've never visited my current bank, but I use their Web site almost every day. I also drive by my old bank every day.

I'm just curious. Does your church have a Web site?

WHAT CAME FIRST?

Brand Autopsy once launched a series of posts taking an inside look at Starbucks. Mr. Brand Autopsy, John Moore, used to be the retail marketing manager at Starbucks, so he offered a unique perspective on a rapidly growing company.

In the first post, he made a fantastic point about brands. He said, "You cannot create a brand before you create a business. Your business creates your brand. Your brand should never create your business." For Starbucks, that means they were more focused on roasting the highest quality beans and creating welcoming places for people to enjoy coffee. John suggests "the by-product was the creation of a strong brand."[53]

TONY MORGAN

The same holds true in ministry. You should be primarily focused on your mission to fulfill the Great Commission and the Great Commandment. Out of that mission may come a commitment to strategies like relevant teaching, quality experiences for adults and kids, innovative approaches to worship and the arts, etc. And if you do that well, the way you fulfill your mission may create a very strong "brand" within your community. In other words, people will begin to form perceptions of what they're going to experience before they ever step foot on your campus.

The point is that you shouldn't begin with those "desired perceptions" and then decide to commit to relevant teaching, excellence in first impressions, and innovative worship experiences. Begin with your passion for Jesus and your commitment to the mission that God has placed on your church to help people become fully devoted followers of Christ. Out of that will come the teaching, the worship, and ultimately your church's brand—the intangibles including the perceptions of the experience that people associate with your ministry.

I'm still not sure if the chicken or the egg came first, but I do know you can't begin with the brand.

WHAT DO THEY HEAR?

For several years of my ministry, I got to hang out with Kem Meyer (kemmeyer.com), the communications director for Granger Community Church. Here are some questions I heard Kem ask in a keynote conference session that I think every church should consider:

- Who are you talking to, and why should those people spend their time and attention on your church?
- What is your church doing to reduce the noise in people's lives? Or are you just adding to their junk mail?
- What are the barriers that are preventing people from taking their next step?
- Rather than asking "What do we need to tell them?" (more about us), ask "What do they need to know?" (more about them).
- Are you trying to make life easier for your staff/team instead of for your audience/guests?
- What can people get at your church they can't get elsewhere (and we're not talking about other churches)?
- Are you doing it because it works, or because it's cool?
- Are you regularly saying "no"?
- Can you maintain it? (If not, that's an instance when you really should say no.)[54]

Periodically it's important to step back and review what you're communicating through words and actions and how it's being communicated. And more important, rather than evaluating what you're saying, you should really be determining what it is that people are actually hearing.

WHY I BLOG

- Blogging helps me network with thought leaders from throughout the world. (OK, there may be one or two thought laggards as well. You know who you are.)

TONY MORGAN

- It provides a way for me to record what's happening in my journey through life. I've never had a journal until now.
- I get to join the dialogue on how leadership, communications, and ministry will be shaped going forward.
- It may not be reality but for my ego's sake, let's just assume blogging gives me some influence.
- It creates an easy way for me to search through thoughts I had months ago. I have a bad memory, so being able to Google my thoughts has been beneficial.
- It forces me to remain disciplined in my reading and research.
- It offers an opportunity for others to challenge my thinking. Some people even do that in a way that is biblically appropriate.
- I process what I believe and figure out who I am while I write. I think; therefore, I blog.
- People send me free stuff.
- It provides me a platform to share what's happening behind the scenes at NewSpring and to challenge other churches to consider new ministry strategies for impacting today's culture.
- It offers an opportunity for me to put a face and a personality on the "strategic" side of ministry. I know. It's hard to believe I used "personality" and "strategic" in the same sentence.
- It forces me to be on the leading edge of what's happening in our culture.
- I express my thoughts and feelings better in writing than

I do verbally. (I think I just heard my wife, Emily, shout an "Amen!")

- It makes it easier for me to respond to others who have questions or need information about NewSpring or my ministry. I can just point them to a post on my blog. And then, I'm answering the same question for more people.
- It allows me to update friends and family on what's happening in my life. Yes, there are people who actually care.
- People I really respect have blogs.
- I enjoy trying to help people laugh more and enjoy life. I laugh more when I blog. That's healthy for me.
- My mom likes it.

WHY SHOULD I ATTEND?

How do you encourage someone to attend your church for the first time? Do you tell them how great your church is? Or do you tell them how the experience may impact their life?

Kathy Sierra from Creating Passionate Users offers a foundational lesson on how we need to communicate with people who are deciding whether or not to attend our churches. If you hear nothing else, remember this: "Quit telling us how great you are, and start telling us how you plan to deliver something that helps the user become greater."[55]

TONY MORGAN

THE WIFE WHISPERER

So I'm at the ballpark one evening watching my son play baseball. I'm just minding my own business. Then without any provocation, my wife puts her hand on my shoulder and leans over to whisper in my ear. She said . . .

Wait a second. You're certainly not interested in what my wife had to say, are you? You probably just read my writings for the leadership and ministry insights I share. You certainly wouldn't be reading to keep up with my wife's ballpark banter, would you?

Just so you know. What she said is probably not what you're thinking she said. It *could* be what you're thinking, but it's probably *not* what you're thinking. If you're really nice to me, though, and you really want to know, I might be willing to share her secret.

Through the years I've discovered that my audience apparently doesn't love me for my brain. You appear to get the most gratification peering into the mysterious crevices of my life. You are an Oprah-watching, *People* magazine-reading crowd that is satisfied with overtly gawking as a man bares his soul. That said, now for the good stuff. My wife put her hand on my shoulder, leaned over, and whispered into my ear, "So when are you going to get a BlackBerry?" My heart just melted. I thought, "My wife is so cool. She not only knows the latest and greatest technology—she also wants me to own it." All I can say is that Emily earned quite a few "points" with that simple question. And it got me to thinking. What are the other things I wish my wife would say to me? With that in mind, here are:

✦ ✦ 10 MORE THINGS I WISH MY WIFE ✦ ✦
WOULD WHISPER INTO MY EAR

1. I think you'd look best in the black Nissan Z350.
2. I've been thinking that we need to watch more ESPN together.
3. Today's your day, and you don't need to do any cooking or laundry.
4. It's OK, I'm sure most men don't know how to change a furnace filter.
5. Biceps are so overrated.
6. How do you get the lines in the lawn so straight?
7. You, sir, could write the book on *Simply Strategic Conversations*.
8. I think you need a bigger television.
9. He has more subscribers, but you're my favorite blogger.
10. We need to eat more pizza.

As a pastor and leader, doing what it takes to maintain a healthy marriage relationship is just about one of the most important things I can do. *Without* a healthy marriage, my ministry is over. So if you get the sense from reading some of these sections that I must really love my wife—well, the fact is, I do. But I don't take that for granted. I know without God's protection and a plan to maintain the health of our marriage, it could all come to an end. And that's part of the reason why I listen very closely to what my wife has to say—even the little secrets she whispers into my ear.

TONY MORGAN

WIN A HARLEY!

Someone at Crossroads Church (crossroadschurch.com) in Corona, California, recently found themselves in "Hawg Heaven" when the church drew his name as the winner of a brand new Harley Davidson motorcycle.

Crossroads was celebrating the grand opening of their new 3,000-seat auditorium, and in their message series, "Adventures in Friendship," they used the Harley giveaway as an incentive to attract first-time visitors to the church. First-time visitors or members who brought first-time visitors were entered into the drawing to win the Harley.

Crossroads used the giveaway to encourage evangelism and outreach to the community. Pastor Barry McMurtrie explained, "Our goal is to become a community gathering place, and this program supports that vision!"[56]

So I guess if you happen to be in Corona, California, you may want to visit Crossroads and see if they're holding any big drawings. It may be your turn to go "Hawg Wild."

WORSHIP MUSIC

One of my friends in ministry, who is also a lurker on my blog, e-mailed me with a question. This one should generate some conversation. And for that reason, he's chosen to remain nameless. Let's just call him "Mr. Nameless Lurker Ministry Guy." Here's what Mr. Nameless Lurker Ministry Guy had to say:

"I'm curious to know if you are aware of any posts on blogs or articles or books that address progressive, cutting-edge worship music/styles. In my search on the Internet, I seem to be able to find a lot of people that are all saying the same stuff, and quite frankly, it's very boring. It has a grain of truth but seems to lack thorough logic and misses all consideration for unchurched people. Do you know of anyone addressing cutting edge, progressive worship?"

Here are a few observations I'll offer. Generally speaking, worship music doesn't sound like the music I hear on the Top 40 radio channels. I would obviously expect the *lyrics* to be different, but stylistically, contemporary worship music sounds very, well—Christian. Does worship music necessarily have to be slower, contemplative music? Is it possible to express worship in music using up-tempo, more energetic songs?

Should we be more sensitive to the lyrics of the worship songs we use when our services are trying to connect with people who are unchurched? For example, one of my favorite worship songs is "Marvelous Light" by Charlie Hall. Even though I love the song, I'm wondering whether or not the lyrics may be too confusing for someone who's unchurched. For example: "I once was fatherless, a stranger with no hope," or "Your love it beckons deeply, a call to come and die," or "My dead heart now is beating, my deepest stains now clean." Is it possible to worship God while remaining sensitive to people who are not yet Christ followers?

I think our worship music has become more about us than about God. We're creating songs that only make sense to *us* (though some of it *I* don't even understand) using a style that's foreign to our culture. I don't think my faith (or my worship) is supposed to be about me. My main objective in life is

TONY MORGAN

to love God and love others. Shouldn't my life and my worship make sense to both God and others?

Is it possible that music could exist for us to worship God while at the same time being stylistically appealing and lyrically understandable for the unchurched? Or are we always going to have our version of "hymns" that only appeal to a segment of our Christian culture?

With that, Mr. Nameless Lurker Ministry Guy decided to reengage in the conversation. Here are his continuing thoughts:

I obviously understand an unbeliever cannot worship God. However, "unchurched" does not mean "unbeliever." I've been a Christ follower since I was a child. However, there was a period of my life when I was "unchurched," or as some call it, "de-churched." Regardless, the church is the bride of Christ. A bride is supposed to be attractive, put together, every detail in order, pure, etc. I think this should encompass all that we do, including our music. So here are some random thoughts and questions.

Many pastors of contemporary churches prepare and deliver their sermons in a way that will connect with non-Christians *and* with Christians. Is it possible for our worship music to do the same? I think the lyrics are important for believers. However, the quality and style of the music is something that can connect with all, regardless of the lyrics. So a non-believer should be able to come to our churches and be surprised and thrilled with the quality and style of the music, regardless of lyrics." (**TONY SAYS**: I don't think it's a secret that I'm in agreement with Mr. Lurker here.)

Also, isn't it odd that during the week I listen to all kinds of music (classic rock, alternative rock, European rock, country) and then I show up to church on the weekend and listen to a different style of music called "praise and worship"? Can't I worship God with a style of music that I like and is of high quality? (**TONY SAYS**: I may have to distance myself from Mr. Lurker if he occasionally listens to country music.)

Are Christian musicians creative enough to create a new, cutting-edge style of music? Are we only capable of imitating what's already been created? (**TONY SAYS**: I think we're already seeing this in some churches.)

When are any Christian musicians going to start writing lyrics that connect with the average Joe? For example, I can't imagine hearing two men say to each other, 'I just want my lifesong to sing to God' and the reply, 'Yes, I just feel like my heart is crying out.' When will we have lyrics that are about real life? I understand that poetry and poetic lyrics are cool and all, but you know what I'm saying. (**TONY SAYS**: Amen! Today's worship music isn't very manly.)

Isn't it possible to worship God without saying or hearing a word? Doesn't the Bible talk about making a joyful *noise*? Isn't a noise most likely a note rather than a lyric? Of course, lyrics are also mentioned in the

Bible, so I'm not discounting the importance of them. (**TONY SAYS**: I don't know that there's disagreement in the conversation on this point.)

Is worship about who we are, or is it about who God is? Or is it both? (**TONY SAYS**: I'd say both, if we follow David's example in the Psalms.)

How do we measure our worship? Are we only effective if the audience/congregation is standing for the entire music set? Or if they are clapping, dancing, etc.? I'm pretty sure I've worshiped on my own, in my car, sitting down, without saying a word. (**TONY SAYS**: Again, we're assuming that we all agree worship is far more than singing. But if we were focusing just on the singing, what do you think of Mr. Lurker's comments?)

How important is the flow of music? How important is the emotion of the music? What about the ebb and flow of a combination of songs? Changes of tempo? Moments of just instrumentals? Maybe moments of silence? (**TONY SAYS**: Important.)

I can hear the pushback already. "This is about worship music. It's about believers worshiping God through music. It doesn't matter if the style of the music is unfamiliar to unbelievers. It doesn't matter if unbelievers don't understand the words. The worship isn't for them—it's for God."

Well, that's just partially correct. When Paul wrote to the Christians in Corinth, he cautioned them to consider the reaction of unbelievers when the church gathers. Check this out:

So where does it get you, all this speaking in tongues no one understands? It doesn't help believers, and it only gives unbelievers something to gawk at. Plain truth-speaking, on the other hand, goes straight to the heart of believers and doesn't get in the way of unbelievers. If you come together as a congregation and some unbelieving outsiders walk in on you as you're all praying in tongues, unintelligible to each other and to them, won't they assume you've taken leave of your senses and get out of there as fast as they can? But if some unbelieving outsiders walk in on a service where people are speaking out God's truth, the plain words will bring them up against the truth and probe their hearts. Before you know it, they're going to be on their faces before God, recognizing that God is among you. (1 Cor. 14:22–25 MSG)

How we worship is important because it could potentially impact the response of people who attend our services but aren't yet Christ followers. If Paul had such strong caution about speaking with "unintelligible" words, it doesn't seem like a huge leap to suggest we need to be sensitive to unbelievers with the lyrics we sing. If *that* doesn't convince you, ask yourself if God is less "worshiped" when the way we worship is understandable to everyone present? If not, why wouldn't we be sensitive to those in our services who haven't committed their lives to Christ? God evidently has a heart for people who are lost (see Matthew 18 as an example). If that's his heart, seems like it should be ours as well.

TONY MORGAN

YELLING AT THE TELEVISION

I'm a sports nut. Doesn't really matter what season it is, my television is frequently tuned into the big game. Here's what I've learned through the years, though—I can yell at the television all I want, but it's not going to change the outcome of the game. I have no influence from my family room. I'm a spectator. No matter how loud I yell, I'm not going to change whether or not my team wins the game.

The irony, from my perspective, is that we Christ followers seem to be just yelling at the television. We're angry. I think we're fearful. We know the world around us is slipping away, yet all we are doing is yelling at the boob tube. We're certainly not in the game. We won't go there. It's too messy. It's dirty. It's uncomfortable. Life, that is. It's all around us. It's real and it's raw. We're afraid to engage the culture. We prefer to yell at it. And ironically, the louder we yell, the less the world listens. We must look like idiots screaming at the big, blue screen.

It doesn't need to be like that. The church can still engage this culture. We don't have to sit by, waiting for the outcome of the game. We can actually participate. In fact, I think we can still influence the outcome. Yes, I said the church can influence the culture.

The challenge, of course, is that we can't wait for the world around us to get saved and come to us. We have to start a conversation that shows we understand the reality of life. We have to demonstrate that we understand this dialogue doesn't begin with perfection—it begins with relational heartache, addictions, physical needs, financial crisis, hopelessness, and lots of questions. We have to get the culture's attention. We have to speak their language. We have to address their questions. If we don't, we'll be talking to ourselves. We may feel holy, but we'll leave those around us feeling empty.

Paul said it this way, "I kept my bearings in Christ—but I entered their world and tried to experience things from their point of view. I've become just about every sort of servant there is in my attempts to lead those I meet into a God-saved life" (1 Cor. 9:22 MSG).

Paul engaged his culture to win people to Jesus Christ, and we must do the same today. We must address their needs and their questions before we can impose our agenda. We need to stop yelling at the television and dare to actually get in the game. Then and only then will we have the opportunity to help make the kingdom of God real for the world around us.[57]

YOU HAVE MY ATTENTION

As I share this, my daughter Brooke is only twenty-six months old. She does know how to communicate, though—especially to her father. In recent weeks, when she senses I'm getting ready to leave the house to go off to work, she'll confidently say, "Kiss me, Daddy." I melt every time she says it. And I always respond and willingly give her what she's asked for.

Just in case you're wondering, there's power in simple utterances to the father.

TONY MORGAN

YOUR BILLBOARDS DON'T WORK

Remember the old days when every phone that you owned had the alphabet listed from A to Z above each of the numbers you used for dialing? That's so yesterday. My smartphone has a QWERTY keyboard. In other words, every letter has its own button. That's a great feature until you're driving down the highway and see a billboard that says something like this: "Buy our superior product. Call 1-800-UR-STUCK." (Don't really call that. I made it up.)

What do you do when you own a Blackjack cell phone like me? You don't respond to the ad because it's impossible to dial the phone number.

I was amazed today on my drive home from the beach at how many billboards and vehicles are plastered with telephone numbers that I can't call. Even though my smartphone is too dumb to call their telephone numbers, I could have used it to surf their Web sites. Only I couldn't do that either because a number of those same ads didn't include a Web address.

When you have a chance, it might be a good idea to make sure your audience can respond to your message.

YOUR MESSAGE

- I want to hear your heart and not your brain.
- If you listen to me, I *may* listen to you.
- At best, I'll remember one thing you say.
- Your message is only one of thousands I've already heard today.

KILLING COCKROACHES

- When you admit you've messed up, it reminds me that you're real.
- I'm not convinced it's truth.
- I'm moved by stories.
- When you make me laugh, I engage.
- I hear it, but sometimes I need to see it or feel it or experience it.
- I'm watching to see if you keep your promise.
- I think it's funny that you still think you control your message.
- Polished scares me.
- In order to speak to me, you can't speak to everyone.
- I'm not impressed by big words.
- If it's not about me, then I'm not listening.
- Your message has more impact when you shorten it.
- It's OK if you don't have an answer for everything.
- What are *your* questions?
- Your message has impact if someone disagrees.
- You'd be wise to participate in our online conversation.
- I know it seems awkward, but it helps me when you repeat the important stuff.
- Your message is not for you.
- I don't have to listen to you.

YUCK

Emily has proclaimed from the early days that she would never become a short order cook. She doesn't take orders from me or the kids and whip up whatever we want to eat whenever we want to eat it. Instead she prepares a meal (she's a great cook, by the way) and we eat whatever she prepares.

With the kids, we basically give them a choice. They can eat what's in front of them, or they don't have to eat. I know. Some may say we're bad parents. However, we learned that kids will always eat when they're hungry. And by not giving them meal options, they've learned to enjoy all sorts of food.

But as you can imagine, there are still some foods they don't prefer. Here's where the second rule comes into play. We don't allow our kids to say, "I don't like this." Or, "Yuck." Or, "This food makes me want to vomit." Because we want our kids growing up thinking more about the cook than themselves, we have encouraged them to use the phrase, "This is not my favorite."

This morning, after the three older kids had left for school and Emily and I were getting ready for the day, Brooke, our youngest, had the opportunity to watch her one episode of Dora the Explorer. Brooke is a Dora addict. At times she'll just blurt out the word "map" for no apparent reason.

Unfortunately this morning there was a snafu with the Dora episode that had been recorded on the DVR. It stopped mid-adventure. Emily went into the family room to get things figured out. As she was trying to get Dora going again, the news channel was giving an update on last night's election results. Brooke soaked in the news update for a few moments and then stated, "This is not my favorite."

With that, Brooke has cast her vote for Dora to be the next president of the United States.

(JUST ONE MORE . . .)
WHEN YOU THINK YOU'RE RIGHT

I have a growing frustration. It's something that's been on my mind for the last several months. Maybe you can help me out here.

I'm always fascinated by people who have their perspective of the right way to do church. And rather than just doing church the way they believe is the right way, they feel like they have to tell other churches why they're doing it the wrong way. Why is that?

In fact, if someone figured out the right way to do church and wanted to try to encourage other churches to consider that right way, even that would make sense. I'd likely listen and learn from what they have to say. But instead of doing that, I've seen many instances when people feel like they need to attack churches that do it differently.

Here's what I'm saying. If you think the answer to fulfilling the Great Commission is home churches, then go do home churches. If the answer to reaching people for Jesus is being more missional, then go be more missional. If the answer is avoiding any reference to today's culture and eliminating "secular" music or drama or video illustrations, then launch a church that embraces those values. If the answer is creating seeker-sensitive or purpose-driven ministries or church planting or multisite, then do that. No one is stopping you. Hopefully this will be freeing to you. Consider this:

- God is sovereign. If it's consistent with his design, he'll bless it.

- If people accept Christ and experience new life, I will celebrate with you.
- If God blesses your ministry, you should share the good news with others.
- If God blesses your ministry, you should also encourage others and help them learn from your successes.
- I'm not stopping you. I'm not creating barriers. If God's telling you to do it, you should do it. You don't need my approval. Really—you should do it.
- I won't attack your church because it's different from mine. It would really be nice if you'd show me the same courtesy.

Here's my encouragement to you: Don't condemn others because others are different than you. Don't create division. Do what God tells you to do.

ACKNOWLEDGMENTS

I've had the privilege of serving in ministry for more than ten years in two great churches. There's no question that the insights and strategies included in this book are a reflection of the influence (and patience) of my friends in ministry from both Granger and NewSpring. A special debt of gratitude goes to Perry Noble, though, for allowing me the time and the freedom to pursue my passion with this book.

My mind is being stretched daily by fellow bloggers like Mark Batterson, Joshua Blankenship, Penelope Trunk, Tim Stevens, Craig Groeschel, Bobby Gruenewald, Kathy Sierra (in her former life), John Moore, Carlos Whittaker, Scott Hodge, Seth Godin, and Guy Kawasaki. If you're thinking, "That thought sounds familiar," it probably is. I love my blog-roll.

Over the last few years, I've also had a number of friends join the dialogue at tonymorganlive.com. Your comments, questions, wisdom, challenging thoughts, and encouragement have certainly shaped the content and flavor of this book. (But, no, I'm not going to share the royalties with you.)

I'd like to thank Shane Duffey, Scott Hodge, Jennifer Jones, Tim Magnuson, Kem Meyer, Mark Meyer, Emily Morgan (the best and hottest editor in the world), Sydney Olin, Jeff Pelletier, Jami Ruth, and Tim Stevens for their review and feedback on the beta version of this book.

B&H Publishing Group took a risk with this one. I certainly want to thank editor Tom Walters and the entire team, including Jeff Godby, Greg Pope, Kim Stanford, Andrea Dennis, and Lawrence Kimbrough. You made me sound wiser and

TONY MORGAN

look sharper than I really am. Thanks for helping to set this project up for success.

My foundation as a leader started at home. I get many of my strengths (and my quirks) from my parents, Jerrel and Mary-Jo. They instilled the drive and creativity and passion that God is refining.

My wife, Emily, and our kids, Kayla, Jacob, Abby and Brooke, are the ones that are really writing the story. They make me laugh. They make me think. They bring me joy. I'm one lucky (or if you prefer "blessed") man.

This book, though, is dedicated to Emily. Thank you for helping me be who God designed me to be. I hope I'm returning the favor.

NOTES

1. Barbara Whiting, "How to Kill Cockroaches in Your Home," About.com, Inc., http://homeparents.about.com/cs/householdtips/ht/cockroaches.htm.

2. John Moore, "Another Wal-Mart Feel-Good Story," September 12, 2005, http://brandautopsy.typepad.com/brandautopsy/2005/09/more_walmart_fe.html.

3. Technorati.com, April 18, 2008, http://technorati.com/about.

4. Enid Burns, "Clarity on Best Day to E-Mail," August 16, 2006, http://clickz.com/showpage.html?page=3623180.

5. Kathy Sierra, "Passionate Users Talk Different," December 11, 2005, http://headrush.typepad.com/creating_passionate_users/2005/12/passionate_user.html.

6. Kevin D. Hendricks, "Lessons from Seeker Sensitive Churches," April 25, 2005, www.churchmarketingsucks.com/archives/2005/04/lessons_from_se.html.

7. Enid Burns, "Funny, Multi-Channel Campaigns Reach College Students," July 20, 2006, www.clickz.com/showpage.html?page=3622907.

8. Originally published as a "Web Exclusive" by *Outreach* magazine, July/August 2006, www.outreachmagazine.com/library/webexclusives/06julaugwebexmorgancompel.asp.

9. John Moore, "Advance Studies Into Starbucks-ology," December 17, 2006, http://brandautopsy.typepad.com/brandautopsy/2006/12/advance_studies.html.

10. Tony Morgan and Tim Stevens, Loveland, CO: Group Publishing, 2005, 45.

11. "What's Your Optimism Ratio?" February 25, 2005, www.stevepavlina.com/blog/2005/02/whats-your-optimism-ratio.

12. "In Praise of the Purple Cow," *Fast Company*, Issue 67, January 2003, 74.

13. Emanuel Rosen, *The Anatomy of Buzz* (New York: Doubleday, 2000), 181–83.

14. John C. Maxwell, *The 21 Irrefutable Laws of Leadership* (Nashville: Thomas Nelson, 1998), 126.

15. William C. Taylor and Polly LaBarre, *Mavericks at Work* (New York: William Morrow, 2006), xiv.
16. Originally published as a "Web Exclusive" by *Outreach* magazine, March/April 2007, www.outreachmagazine.com/ library/webexclusives/ma07webextonymorgan.asp.
17. Scott Rodgers, "Guest Blog: Scott Rodgers," June 5, 2007, http://swerve.lifechurch.tv/2007/06/05/ guest-blog-scott-rodgers.
18. Josh Griffin, "Movie Review: Spider-Man 3," May 6, 2007, www.morethandodgeball.com/?p=1743.
19. Robert McMillan, "Loosen the Reins, Says Google CEO," InfoWorld.com, May 19, 2005, www.infoworld.com/ article/05/05/19/HNloosenreins_1.html.
20. Brian Tome, "Fresh Breath: Prayer Is Natural," July 7, 2005, http://crazychurch.com/talks/showarticle.uplx?articleid=255.
21. Mark Memmott, "It's A New Look For USATODAY.Com," March 3, 2007, http://blogs.usatoday.com/ondeadline/ 2007/03/welcome_to_the_.html#more.
22. Fred Vogelstein, "Text Of Wired's Interview With Google CEO Eric Schmidt," April 9, 2007, www.wired.com/techbiz/people/ news/2007/04/mag_schmidt_trans?currentpage=1.
23. Steven Levitt, "Cut God Some Slack," August 2, 2007, http://freakonomics.blogs.nytimes.com/2007/08/02/ cut-god-some-slack.
24. Originally published as a "Web Exclusive" by *Outreach* magazine, May/June 2006, www.outreachmagazine.com/ library/webexclusives/06mayjnwebexmorgan.asp.
25. Kevin Hendricks, "Poll Results: How Cool Is Your Church Web Site?" September 12, 2005, www.churchmarketingsucks.com/ archives/2005/09/poll_results_ho_1.html.
26. Lucas Graves, "America's Next Top Network?" *Wired*, October 2006.
27. Matt Friedeman, "A Youth Exodus from Church—What Are We Doing Wrong?" AgapePress, August 14, 2006.
28. Originally published as a "Web Exclusive" by *Outreach* magazine, November/December 2007, www.outreach magazine.com/library/insights/nd07webextonymorgan.asp.

29. "Online Extra: Jeff Bezos on Word-of-Mouth Power," August 2, 2004, www.businessweek.com/magazine/content/04_31/B3894101.htm.

30. Originally published as a "Web Exclusive" by *Outreach* magazine, November/December 2006, www.outreach magazine.com/library/webexclusives/06novdecwebex morganservices.asp.

31. Cabletelevision Advertising Bureau, "MTV Network Profile," www.onetvworld.org/tmpls/network/06profiles/409.pdf.

32. Cabletelevision Advertising Bureau, "MTV Network Profile, 2002, www.cabletvadbureau.com/02profiles/mtvprof.htm.

33. Matt Friedeman, "A Youth Exodus from Church—What Are We Doing Wrong?" AgapePress, August 14, 2006.

34. The Barna Group, "Generational Differences," www.barna.org/flexpage.aspx?page=topic&topicid=22.

35. Lillian Kwon, "Survey: High School Seniors 'Graduating From God'," *The Christian Post*, August 10, 2006.

36. Ibid.

37. Jeremy Hunt, "Interview: The Fray," *Relevant* Magazine, September/October 2006, www.relevantmagazine.com/pc_article.php?id=7248.

38. Gene Weingarten, "Pearls before Breakfast," *Washington Post*, April 8, 2007, W10, www.washingtonpost.com/wp-dyn/content/article/2007/04/04/AR2007040401721.html.

39. Robert Scoble, "No Strategy Is a Strategy," May 27, 2007, http://radio.weblogs.com/ 0001011/2005/05/27.html#A10225.

40. Christopher Percy Collier, "The Expert On Experts," *Fast Company*, November 2006, www.fastcompany.com/magazine/110/final-word.html.

41. Joe Schimmels, "What You Will Not Find in the Church," November 17, 2006, http://revunplugged.blogs.com/unplugged/2006/11/what_you_will_n.html.

42. Kathy Sierra, "Be Provocative," September 13, 2006, http://headrush.typepad.com/creating_passionate_ users/2006/09/be_provocative.html.

43. Michael Hyatt, "What's The Secret To Your Success?" February 27, 2006, www.michaelhyatt.com/workingsmart/2006/02/whats_the_secre.html.

44. Thom Rainer, "To Build or Not to Build?" *Outreach*, September/October 2005, www.outreachmagazine.com/library/insights/05septoctrainersurprisinginsight.asp.

45. Originally published as a "Web Exclusive" by *Outreach* magazine, May/June 2007, www.outreachmagazine.com/library/webexclusives/mj07webextonymorgan.asp.

46. Michael Dell, Abilene Christian University videoconference, February 8, 2005, www.dell.com/downloads/global/corporate/speeches/msd/2005_02_08_msd_acu.pdf.

47. Mya Frazier, "Wal-Mart Tries to Be MySpace, Seriously," *Advertising Age*, July 17, 2006, http://adage.com/abstract.php?article_id=110520.

48. Originally published as a "Web Exclusive" by *Outreach* magazine, July/August 2007, www.outreachmagazine.com/library/webexclusives/ja07webexmorgan.asp.

49. Sheena S. Iyengar and Mark R. Lepper, www.columbia.edu/~ss957/whenchoice.html.

50. Barry Schwartz, *The Paradox of Choice* (New York: Ecco, 2003), 2.

51. Bruce Johnson, "To Bore or Not to Bore," August 26, 2005, http://bruced.typepad.com/brucedjohnsoncom/2005/08/to_bore_or_not_.html.

52. Taylor Clark, "Star B*#!Ked," *Psychology Today*, September/October 2007, 99–102.

53. John Moore, "Building the Business Creates the Brand," October 3, 2005, http://brandautopsy.typepad.com/brandautopsy/2005/10/building_the_bu.html.

54. Kem Meyer, "Are You Talkin' To Me?" Speech at MinistryCom Conference In Houston, September 16, 2005.

55. Kathy Sierra, "Users Don't Care If You Are the Best." May 2, 2005, http://headrush.typepad.com/creating_passionate_users/2005/week18/index.html.

56. Crossroads Christian Church of Corona, press release, April 2, 2005.

57. Reprinted by permission, *REV!* magazine, Copyright 2006, Group Publishing, Inc., Box 481, Loveland, CO 80539.

✦ ✦ **ALSO BY TONY MORGAN** ✦ ✦ ✦

Books
Simply Strategic Growth
Simply Strategic Volunteers
Simply Strategic Stuff

Blogs
tonymorganlive.com (daily insights)
twitter.com/tpmorgan (mini-insights)

Articles
There are forty-some and counting. (Do I have to do everything for you? That's why God created Google.)

TONY MORGAN